PUNCH
Goes to War 1939-1945

To my mother, Betty Coombs Walasek, Leading Aircraftwoman in the WAAF

Thanks to Andre Gailani of Punch Cartoon Library and the team at Topfoto for all their help

Published in 2010 by Prion
An imprint of the Carlton Publishing Group
20 Mortimer Street
London W1T 3JW

1 3 5 7 9 10 8 6 4 2

A CIP catalogue record for this book is available from the British Library.

ISBN 978 1 85375 769 3

Printed in Dubai

*" I'm not going to have people
turning round and blaming* ME *if we
don't win this damned war. "*

PUNCH
Goes to War 1939-1945

Edited by

Helen Walasek

Foreword by

Griff Rhys Jones

CONTENTS

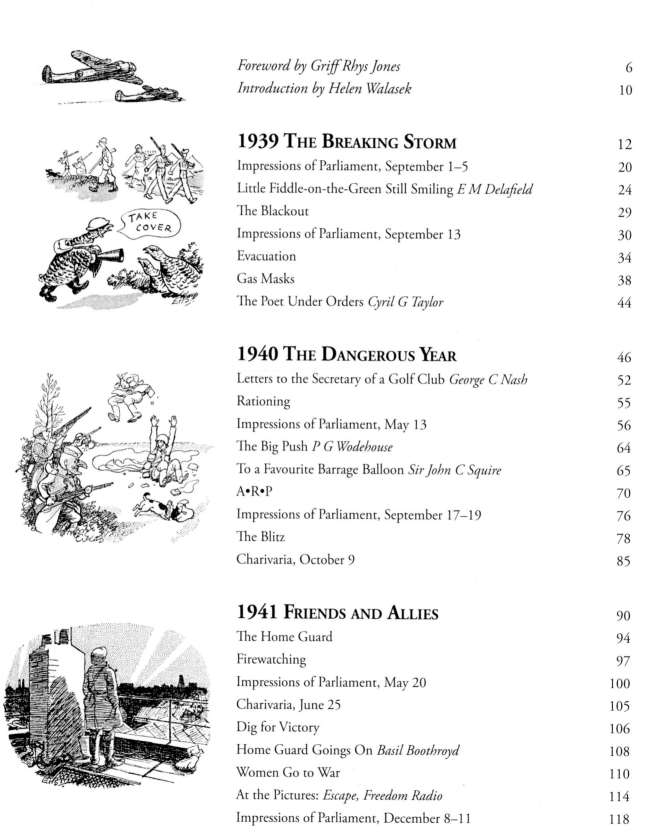

FOREWORD
by Griff Rhys Jones

Well, here is a treat – two of my favourite things combined in one book: cartoons and war. Not the "Donner und Blitzen, Achtung Tommy!" I preferred aged ten, of course, but an equally enjoyable, if more subtle, pen and ink portrait of the Home Front – deep, slightly mystifying and frankly more accurate than any other account I have encountered.

During the Second World War, not everybody was rushing up the beach with Tom Hanks. The vast majority of the population stayed at home, shrouded in bureaucratic mystery, with modest capabilities and not much knowledge; as spectators to somebody else's war. Here is the average citizen in a nervous time: confused middle-class bankers, determined old ladies and gormless junior soldiers. These are not fanatical people. Or smart. They are not bellicose but they are brave. Their courage is tempered by snobbery, sex, officiousness and silliness as it would always be – far more *Dad's Army* than *The Great Escape*.

I once had to interview George MacDonald Fraser, himself a redoubtable veteran. I wanted to know how he did his incredibly accurate research for the Flashman books. "Old copies of *Punch*," he said simply. I knew precisely the ones he meant. My school library had a huge collection of bound volumes of *Punch*, where Gladstone waved obscure bills and six-line jokes nailed the behaviour of rural deans.

By the 1940s, however, as you will see, *Punch* had been through a revolution. The captions had lost weight. The drawings had become less ponderous. The observation was funnier.

The big "political" cartoons still chart the great events in terms of John Bull, Russian Bears and British Lions and those scarily accurate portraits of Adolf (which must surely have condemned the perpetrators in the event

of invasion) – Hitler buried in a Russian snowdrift, Goering blown up as a balloon over Poland. But each carried an emotional kick. We may shudder at national debt, or election prospects, but the waves of swastikas crashing on the indomitable rock of Britain, or Hitler failing to take account of the British Navy were cries of hope in a frightening time.

The "funnies", however, introduce us to the British who know their place, the British who also serve by standing and waiting – usually in a queue, perhaps for a train, or outside a shop, ready with a cautious, nervous or daft remark. And the most telling of these cartoons is a brilliant sketch by Fougasse. It shows a street before and after the declaration of war. You have to look closely, and then you get it. People are talking to each other. It is as simple as that. The war has killed their natural reserve.

Punch shows how valuable to the British spirit facetiousness really was. Even in the midst of cataclysm there needed to be a sense of proportion and a fervent faith in the ridiculous.

The *Punch* reader was expected to recognise himself as the stout, moustachioed father-figure in the tin hat – an unassuming resolutely ordinary person, who was simply not going to stand for it.

We live in difficult times ourselves. *Punch* is no more. Newspaper editors are cutting their costs by dropping British cartoonists from our daily pages. Who will record us for the future? There are plenty of columnists blathering on. But for all the waffle, will they ever be as vivid as these sharp, accurate, funny miniature scoops of life? We need them.

Griff Rhys Jones
London, September 2010

"Look here, Major, don't you realise that there's a war on?"

No. 5281   PUNCH SUMMER NUMBER—May 18 1942   Volume CCIII

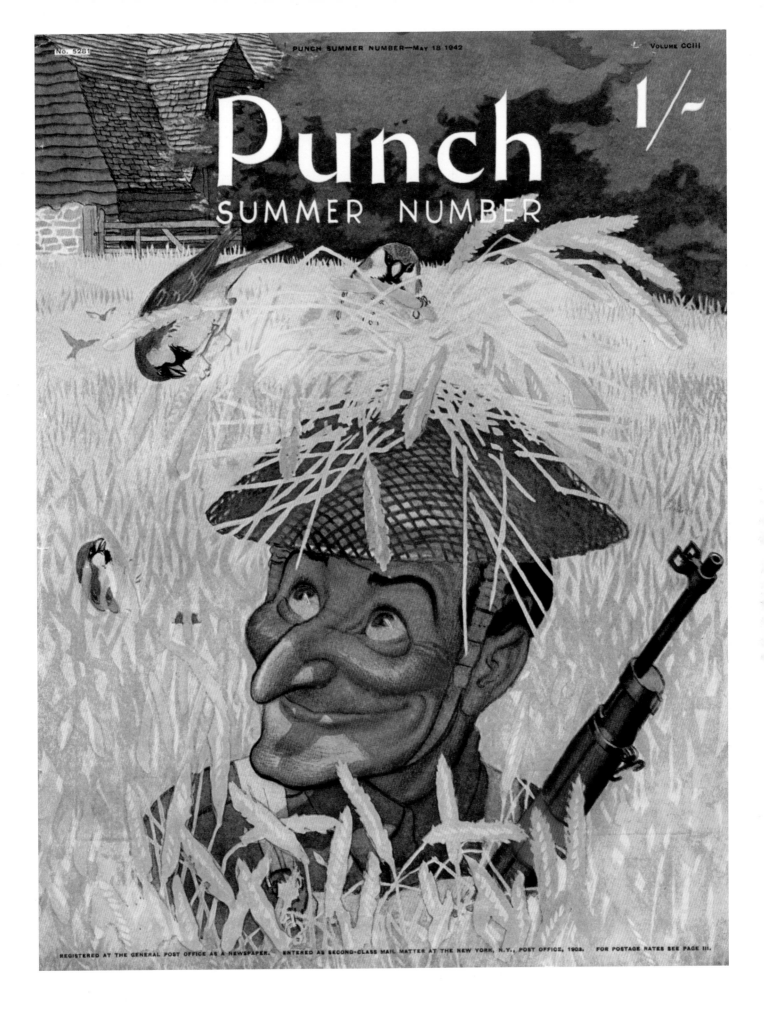

Punch

SUMMER NUMBER

1/-

REGISTERED AT THE GENERAL POST OFFICE AS A NEWSPAPER.   ENTERED AS SECOND-CLASS MAIL MATTER AT THE NEW YORK, N.Y., POST OFFICE, 1902.   FOR POSTAGE RATES SEE PAGE III.

ADOLF IN THE LOOKING GLASS
Herr Hitler. *"How frightful I look to-day!"*

PEACE
"The design's a little odd, but I must say it does look fairly burglar-proof."

THE WAR SALAD
Mussolini. *"Let me see – they say 'A miser for the vinegar, a spendthrift for the oil, and a madman to stir it.' But – is the oil going to hold out?"*

THE SWEETS OF AGGRESSION
Haile Selassie. *"Have I got this right? – He's taken nearly half of what I had and now you gentlemen want to discuss whether he should take any more."*

THE EXPANSIONISTS
"Come on, boys! Let's all make ourselves as big as bulls."

THE GOOSE-STEP
"Goosey Goosey Gander, wither dost thou wander?" "Only through the Rhineland – pray excuse my blunder!"

THE DAWN OF PROGRESS
"But how am I to see it? They've blinded me."

THE STROLLING PLAYERS
France. *"Those two seem to be always walking out on us."* John Bull. *"Well, however awkward it is for the rest of us, the show must go on."*

TWO HEARTS THAT BEAT AS ONE
Frau Germania. *"It is evident to me that colonies are the legitimate sphere of action for Herr Micawber."*

THE FRANCO COMPOSITE AIRCRAFT

The Upper Component. *"Thanks for the lift, but I'm sure you'll agree that I can manage now without your suppport."*

PILLORIED

Japan. *"Do they seriously think this is going to stop me?"*

J'Y SUIS, J'Y RESTE

Mr. Chamberlain. *"I shall wait till it clears up a bit before I get down."*

HIS EASTER EGG

The Fuhrer. *"Excellent – all through!"*

HOMELESS

A Problem for Europe

SCRATCHED

Winston. *"All the same it would have been a winner ... with the right man up."*

NEIGHBOURLY CONDUCT

Herr Hitler. *"Extraordinary how the least little bit of noise seems to upset some parties."*

STILL HOPE

THE DOGS OF PEACE

Voices from the crowd. *"Come on, Number Four!"*

INTRODUCTION
by Helen Walasek

When war was declared on September 3, 1939, *Punch* could have been in no doubt about its role in the conflict. At the beginning of the Great War the magazine had wondered if perhaps there was "no place for humour in a world of horror and mourning…." But it was not long before Mr Punch was convinced "it was not only his privilege but his duty to continue ministering mirth." The magazine, already a national institution, was soon regarded an essential wartime morale-booster – for the officer classes, at least. Thus a 1940 advertisement reminds readers: they had needed *Punch* in the 1914–18 war, and they would certainly need it now.

Punch's editor since 1932, the genial EV Knox – Evoe – agreed with its proprietors, Bradbury & Agnew, to set aside any thoughts of leaving and see the magazine through the war: there were testing times ahead. In December 1944, *Time* magazine visited the *Punch* offices at 10 Bouverie Street ("as gloomy, well-polished,

and oak-paneled as any at Whitehall") and painted a picture of a routine little changed from peacetime. But, of course, everything had changed overnight in 1939. With the threat of German air raids, *Punch* was – quite literally – on the frontline. Bouverie Street was at the heart of London's Fleet Street newspaper district with its stocks of inflammable paper, just minutes from St Paul's Cathedral. The huge incendiary raid of December 29, 1940 unleashed a firestorm that came frighteningly close to *Punch* as both sides of Ludgate Hill were set ablaze. The bombs fell near Bouverie St that night and the Associated Press building around the corner in Tudor St was struck.

On another occasion a gas main in Bouverie Street itself was hit. Evoe found the air raids rather energizing and his assistant editor, HF Ellis, recalled how "he took to wandering about wherever the bombs fell thickest, with a bottle of whisky in his pocket, looking for people who needed it." Evoe arrived at the *Punch* offices the

"... I am beginning to think I have been letting things worry me too much lately, because ..."

morning after the gas mains incident to find publications ranging from *The Economist* to *Little Dot's Playhouse* bombed out and himself unable to smoke because of the leaking gas.

There were no more convivial dinners around the venerable Punch Table, carved with the initials of the magazine's editors and greatest contributors; that had been packed off to safety in one of the Agnews' country homes. While former Sergeant-Major Frampton still guarded the front entrance, it was an entrance protected by sandbags and a sheet of corrugated iron. Dorothy Barker, Evoe's secretary, worked by day and firewatched by night. As the war went on and paper shortages worsened, the magazine's paper became coarser, the print quality blotchier, while the number of pages was cut to 28 – though legend has it *Punch* was considered so essential to the war effort it was granted an extra paper allowance.

Shortly before the war the magazine had been updated with a clean uncluttered look, overseen by its Art Editor Kenneth Bird, the celebrated illustrator Fougasse. The Second World War was to make Fougasse a household name after he offered his services (gratis) to the Ministry of Information and drew its anti-rumour campaign, *Careless Talk Costs Lives*. Bird had been nurturing a clutch of new cartoonists working in a contemporary style, but war was to scatter them across the globe – or at least into work and lives so all-consuming and utterly different from what had gone before that there was little time for drawing. The magazine's star was Pont – Graham Laidler. Already famous for *The British Character*, over the first year of the war Pont produced witty drawings by the score. With his characteristic verve and quirky imagination, he perfectly captured what people were thinking and feeling. But tragedy struck: in November 1940 Pont contracted polio and died within days.

William Sillince, who so beautifully depicted the wartime scene, was still drawing. And the indefatigable David Langdon found time to send in dozens of cartoons though he began the war in the London Rescue Service and ended it an RAF squadron leader. Posted to the Middle East, William Scully managed to contribute occasionally, as did Norman Mansbridge. Rowland Emett, slogging away at the Air Ministry, was another new boy, and there was Siggs, Anton, Douglas, Mervyn Wilson and Acanthus, alongside old reliables: Reynolds, Stampa and Morrow. Others – like George Adamson – sent in a flurry of cartoons, only to disappear until the war ended. There was a second tragedy when the brilliant Paul Crum (Roger Pettiward) was killed leading a commando troop during the disastrous Raid on Dieppe in 1942. Crum had drawn "I keep thinking it's Tuesday", one of Punch's most enduringly famous cartoons.

Evoe faced difficulties with the big political cartoons – the fluidity of events meant a topic bedded down at the printers on Saturday might be utterly out of date by Monday. With the uncertainty over the long-awaited invasion of Italy in 1943, he kept at the ready a plate of a springing British Lion by Bernard Partridge. The cartoon had its day in the July 14 issue when Evoe made a Saturday morning call to the printers instructing: "Release the Lion".

The elderly Partridge had wanted to retire but, like Evoe, was persuaded to stay. He soldiered on, publishing his final cartoon in July 1945 at the age of 83 and dying a month later. If there was a surfeit of lurching ogre-like Nazi/Teutons, the master could still produce arresting compositions. Second cartoonist was EH Shepard, a lighter touch, but his fertile imagination created extraordinary work when he pulled out the stops. Leslie Illingworth, third cartoonist, drew of one of the war's most dramatic images: *The Combat,* from 1940. His illustration of a solitary British fighter plane confronting the monstrous sky-darkening Nazi foe precipitated a flood of heartfelt letters.

Historian Asa Briggs commented that Second World War *Punch* recaptures the mood of the period perhaps more evocatively than any other source. We've included a colourful miscellany of writing to give the flavour of the time, but it is the cartoons that reveal the era with the greatest immediacy – bringing to life the restrictions, foibles and fears of wartime Britain.

1939
THE BREAKING STORM

"I'm absolutely fed up with peace and war!"

*"The way they be goin' on, Garge, anybody would
think war was inevitable."*

ARP DEPT.
*"I feel sure we could
drive a fire-engine."*

THE CALL TO TRAINING

(With war inevitable, citizens are urged to enrol for National Voluntary
Service in the reserve armed forces or civilian services like Air Raid
Precautions, the Red Cross and the Women's Land Army.)

*"Now you gents mustn't think from what I've been telling yer that the
Prime Minister is habsolutely satisfied with the situation."*

"Harold dear, if you keep making those dreadful faces I'm afraid you'll stay like it."

"Was your husband through the last war?" "He was, my dear,
and I've been through the next one."

"None of your gas-masks for me. If I'm gassed
I'm gassed. D'you get me argument?"

"My dear, it's as safe as houses."

POPULAR MISCONCEPTIONS – DIPLOMACY

"My dear, could you sleep a wink without dear Mr Chamberlain?"

" So I joined the A.F.S."

THE GATHERING OF THE VULTURES

["The whole great Central European area, of which the Bohemian valley and lands are only a segment, will be renovated through the political will of the Fuehrer."—*German Paper*.]

THE POLE STAR AND THE BEAR

(Uniting Danzig (Gdansk), a predominantly German territory in the
midst of Poland, with the Third Reich became Hitler's pretext for
invading Poland. But the Russian Bear stands between him and his goal.)

Impressions of Parliament

Friday, September 1st.—To a crowded House recalled at the unusual time of six o'clock the blacking-out of the windows seemed an ominous prelude to Mr. CHAMBERLAIN's statement.

Even to those who knew their history well enough not to be surprised by the ineptness and brutality so long the weaknesses of German high diplomacy and unlikely to be less pronounced in the ham-like hands of an uneducated paranoiac, the tragic story which the P.M. had to tell was staggering. He described how on August 30th the British Government had dispatched to the Polish and German Governments an appeal to refrain from military action while negotiations were going on; how the Poles were prepared immediately to give a guarantee to this effect, but no reply came from Germany; how the Germans had expected the Poles at a day's notice to send a pleni-potentiary to discuss proposals of which *neither the Polish nor British Governments* had heard until a moment judged too late by the Germans; how the German Foreign Secretary, whose earlier experiences as a wine-tout seem to have left him in-completely equipped for the ordinary decencies of civilised exchange, spoke of the Poles to Sir NEVILE HENDERSON in the most violent terms and refused to ask the Polish Ambassador to visit him; how in these crazy circumstances Britain and France had had no other course but to send what amounted to an ultimatum, though without a specified time-limit, to Berlin. No reply to it had yet been received. We were ready, said Mr. CHAMBERLAIN. Complete mobilisation had begun in all three Services.

Mr. GREENWOOD reaffirmed the entire support of Labour in exter-minating HITLER, whom he described very moderately as the "arch-enemy of mankind" and from whose recent utterances he quoted with great felicity, and Sir ARCHIBALD SINCLAIR again pledged the support of Liberalism.

Later the House voted £500,000,000 on which to start the War, and passed a large number of emergency measures. In the evening these passed through all their stages in the Lords.

Saturday, September 2nd.—Parlia-ment spent an expectant and quite extraordinary day waiting for official news from the Front Bench. The Commons filled in time with Emergency Bills, the chief of which was the Military Service Extension Bill to con-script men from eighteen to forty-one, and the atmosphere in the Chamber grew more and more like that of a first-night at a theatre of importance where the curtain had jammed. Rumour followed rumour about when the P.M. would speak. Tension mounted. At last Mr. CHAMBERLAIN came on, met with cheer upon cheer.

In an electric silence he told the House that no German reply had been received to the British note. It was possible, he thought, that the delay might be due to efforts being made by the Italian Government to arrange a Five-Power conference; but the British Government had no intention of entering on such a conference while their ally Poland was being subjected to invasion.

Mr. GREENWOOD was anxious in case the delay should look like weak-ness. He believed war to be inevitable, and he hoped that by to-morrow the P.M. would be able to be definite. Sir ARCHIBALD SINCLAIR had the utmost confidence in the loyalty of the French, but he asked that an expres-sion of the feeling of urgency of the House should be conveyed to their Government. In a brief reply the P.M. emphatically declared there was no weakening in the French or British attitude, and soon after listening to a moving but not very realistic appeal from Mr. MAXTON to postpone war at almost any cost, the House adjourned.

Sunday, September 3rd.—When the Commons met for its first Sunday session for over a century it did so in the knowledge that we were already at war. Only a few minutes after Mr. CHAMBERLAIN's broadcast at eleven-fifteen, air-raid warnings had sounded; and now he told the House that no reply had been received from Germany to a British ultimatum which had expired at eleven this morning, and that France was making a similar *démarche.* He spoke simply and with great dignity.

Mr. GREENWOOD referred briefly to the change of feeling in one night from a fear that we were weakening to a mood of relief and resolution, and saluted the gallantry of Poland. Sir ARCHIBALD SINCLAIR then did the same for France.

Mr. CHURCHILL followed: "We are fighting to save the whole world from the pestilence of Nazi tyranny and in defence of all that is most sacred to man." Mr. McGOVERN (I.L.P.): "I cannot support this country in this catastrophe. It will be . . . a material-istic struggle for human gain." Mr. LANSBURY pleaded for fair propaganda, and Mr. LLOYD GEORGE gave his support to the Government. Later Mr. HORE-BELISHA promised, pressed by Members of all parties, to take boys between eighteen and twenty as late as possible, and Captain MARGESSON, the Chief Whip, gave an assurance that Parliament would not be evacuated unless Westminster became untenable.

Events in the Lords again moved along parallel lines.

Monday, September 4th.—Indigna-tion over the sinking of the *Athenia* dominated the sittings of both Houses, which found it not only a gross case of murder, but an unbelievably stupid action on the part of Germany, to whom peaceful relations with the United States will grow every day more vital.

Mr. CHURCHILL, warmly cheered on his most popular appointment to the Admiralty, made a statement in which he pointed out that apart from all other considerations Germany had broken her recent promise that in case of war no ship should be sunk before sufficient arrangements had been made for the passengers' security. He announced that the convoy system was being brought into action as quickly as possible.

There was no opposition to the National Registration Bill.

Tuesday, September 5th.—Both Houses got through a lot of useful work, the Commons showing anxiety about the effectiveness of air-raid signals. Mr. P's. R. wishes, in common, he supposes, with many others, that the sound of cars accelerating in bottom-gear bore a less sinister resem-blance to the opening note of sirens.

Wednesday, September 6th.—Sir THOMAS INSKIP, having suffered a sudden translation to Lord CALDECOTE, was installed as Lord Chancellor this afternoon. The translation was prettily worded; and many nice things were also said about the retiring Chancellor, Lord MAUGHAM.

Statements taken from neutral persons, Mr. CHURCHILL told the Commons, agreed that a submarine had torpedoed and shelled the *Athenia* without warning. She had carried no armament. One hundred and twenty-five of her company were still un-accounted for.

Pressed to extend Summer-time, the new Home Secretary, Sir JOHN ANDERSON, agreed to consider the idea. Sir JOHN SIMON announced that in order to strengthen our financial position abroad, gold now held in the Issue Department was to be trans-ferred to the Exchange Account; and the P.M. promised that periodical statements would be made about the progress of the war.

THREE AS ONE

"Let us have faith that Right makes Might and in that faith let us to the end dare to do our duty as we understand it."
Abraham Lincoln at Gettysburg, 1863.

PRIDE

"Miss Stapleton's been telling me how she won the last war by untying knots on parcels instead of cutting the string."

"It says he done it all to save his face. Well, well."

"Muvver says I don't need to bring my gas-mask, Miss, 'cause I ain't got no sense of smell."

"It's an old tradition in the Southern Skirmishers, Private Bideford-Dawlish, that when a Sergeant says 'left turn' one turns to the left."

SOME WAR-TIME WEAKNESSES – SPREADING RUMOURS

Little Fiddle-on-the-Green Still Smiling

I

"*A LA guerre comme à la guerre*," was the rather apposite quotation uttered by Miss Pin, only about five minutes after the *guerre* had started—and one would have had nothing but praise for such a ready grasp of the (international) situation but for feeling that she chose the wrong person to whom to say it.

The recipient of Miss Pin's *mot*—as the Maginot Line calls it—was Mr. Pancatto, and not only Mr. Pancatto, who, as an author, prefers uttering his own *mots* to applauding other people's, but Mr. Pancatto just after he had been insulted by the A.R.P. at Fiddle Magna.

Guided by the example of the Ministry of Information, one will try to give the public an account of the incident, leaving out anything in the nature of information and everything in the nature of Mr. Pancatto's language.

The long day, with its stream of gas-masks, sandbags, stirrup-pumps, dug-outs, volunteers, tin hats, telephone calls and inquiries about air-raid protection for canaries, had drawn to a close.

The quiet twilight hour of blackened windows, special constables, lampless motor-cars, colliding pedestrians and mislaid electric torches had set in. Alone in a dear little room very kindly lent by the Chapel Guild of Ladies sat Mr. Pancatto, taking night-duty at the telephone. As he said himself, it was the first time he'd sat down for weeks.

Towards half-past one in the morning a most extraordinary and almost totally unforeseen thing happened. The telephone bell rang.

With soldierly coolness and promptitude Mr. Pancatto put down the crossword puzzle, sheathed his pencil (or more probably dropped it and it rolled away in whatever direction one would never have thought it *could* roll by all the laws of gravity), and took up the receiver and uttered some official phrase, such as "Hullo!"

In reply he was told that Headquarters was speaking. Reaching for his gas-mask, Mr. Pancatto said very briefly: "Yes?"

And, believe it or not, Mr. Pancatto's Headquarters informed him that he had been rung up in order to make sure that he was awake.

It has proved impossible to get a detailed account of what happened next. If Mr. Pancatto said even five-eighths of the things that he said he said, then why hasn't he been taken away by the police?

The only absolutely certain thing is that he demanded an apology, saying —but surely with more spirit than accuracy—that he should expect one without fail.

And the whole of the next day, instead of seeing about the substitution of a large-size gas-mask in place of a medium-size for the Rectory cook, Mr. Pancatto was asking everybody in Little Fiddle-on-the-Green whether they thought he was just *playing* at war or what?

Everybody of course said No, they didn't think that, and Miss Pin went so far as to add that she wouldn't blame Mr. Pancatto in the least if he simply left the war to get on as best it could without him. Far from that, however, Mr. Pancatto returned to

night-duty at the A.R.P. office—or room lent by the Chapel Guild of Ladies—the very next evening.

He had, there is reason to believe, got to Twenty-eight Down in the crossword puzzle, and the end was in sight, when the telephone bell rang.

"This is A.R.P. Headquarters at Fiddle Magna speaking," said a voice that Mr. Pancatto, on his own declaration, recognised perfectly.

And before Mr. Pancatto could begin to say any of the things that he'd been saying all day, or any of those that he'd prepared through the watches of the night, the voice added:

"We're ringing up to make sure you're there to receive an apology."

E. M. D.

IN CASE YOU ARE SURPRISED

The pages in colour which follow, dedicated to the arrival of autumn, were prepared and printed, as the reader will no doubt understand, before the outbreak of hostilities, and for this reason contain no reference to war conditions and betray no consciousness of the present state of Great Britain either by night or day. Many may feel that they are none the worse for that.

"Good heavens, Tompkins, just look at the light in that cottage window ! ! !"

1

"May I see your identity card?"

2

THE CHANGING FACE OF BRITAIN.

IV. – THE TOWN HALL.

"Another word of complaint, M'm, and I quits civilian life."

"Makes one realise Britain really has drawn the sword, doesn't it?"

"I shall have to dash home when I get down to 'C,' because it will mean that my potatoes are done."

"But you ought to have seen the one that got away."

" ' 'Ere comes the Liberty men, Miss."
" 'Thanks, but I'm waiting for the ones from the 'Undaunted.' "

The Blackout

With well-founded fears of German bombing raids, a total night-time blackout was imposed across Britain two days before war was declared. Streetlights were switched off, while homes and businesses had to prevent any chink of light showing from their windows, with Air Raid Wardens enforcing the regulations zealously. After a surge in accidents, restrictions were slightly relaxed and pedestrians were permitted to use torches – if they could find the batteries. The blackout was modified to a "dim-out" on September 17, 1944 and lifted for good in May 1945.

"There has been an unsuccessful raid on the Firth of Forth...a German submarine is reported to have been sunk in the North Sea...Lord Gort and General..."

"From down here I can see a chink of light through your dining-room curtains quite distinctly."

"Funny – I've never seen that shop before."

"Your move, sir."

Impressions of Parliament

Wednesday, September 13th.—HITLER, whose declaration that he had no desire to make war on women and children has proved as worthless as all his other statements, and who has now like a spoilt child threatened the Poles with organised terrorism for the crime of resisting his will, got a straight warning this afternoon in the Lords. The question of civilians being bombed was raised by Lord MOTTISTONE, and Lord HALIFAX replied that while the British and French Governments had expressed their desire to protect civilians so far as possible, they held themselves free to take any action if similar restraint was not observed on the other side. Loud cheers left no doubt of the approval of the House.

Among the bits of information which filtered through to the Commons at Questiontime were Mr. CHAMBERLAIN'S announcement that a Ministry of Shipping would soon be established, Mr. BURGIN'S that all munitions factories were working at full capacity and were being added to, and Major TRYON'S that when things had settled down he hoped that a letter posted before 5.30 P.M. in London would reach any part of England or Wales the next morning.

The debate, like one's last pair of spectacles, fell into two parts—a fairly comprehensive survey of the situation by the P.M., and general though kindly criticism of the way in which the infant Ministry of Information had made its opening moves.

Mr. CHAMBERLAIN told the House how much he had been pleased at the first meeting yesterday in Paris of the Supreme War Council by the absolute unanimity of opinion between the French and ourselves. He spoke warmly of the loyal reaction of the Dominions, and of the magnificent spirit being shown by the Polish people; and he went on to describe how the three branches of our Services were busily making their preliminary contacts with the enemy. The convoy system was about to begin, and there had already been successes against U-boats; black-outs were to be slightly relaxed; evacuation had been completed, not without raising its own social problems; and hospital facilities were being still further extended. Finally, Mr. CHAMBERLAIN apologised to the Press for the early

THE LIGHT OF CRITICISM

["Persons using torches must take the utmost care to prevent the light from being directed on to the driver of a vehicle."
Black-Out Regulations.]

MR. GREENWOOD AND SIR SAMUEL HOARE

errors of the Ministry of Information. The aim of this Department, he said, must be "to steer between giving information which might help the enemy to defeat and destroy our own troops and withholding information with the risk of creating an impression that terrible things may be happening of which the public has no knowledge."

Mr. GREENWOOD, convinced of the P.M.'s sincerity, yet took a grave view not only of the major incident of the week, in which police had raided newspapers on Monday night to suppress news of the B.E.F. in France which had already been officially passed out and which later in the night was once more sanctioned, but also of the poor quality of our news service to Dominion and neutral countries, some of the latter, he declared, having already turned in desperation to German sources.

Sir ARCHIBALD SINCLAIR agreed, emphasising the duty of the Ministry to enlighten as well as to suppress. "The Press," he said, "should be given every opportunity of filling up the gap of ignorance which is growing between the public and the Government."

In reply Sir SAMUEL HOARE was honest with the House. He admitted the mistakes which had been made, but pleaded quite reasonably that the strain on the new organisation had been immense. In the immediate future, he prophesied, decided improvement would be shown; and as an instance of the way in which the news service to neutral countries was being expanded he cited the loosening of the censorship so as to allow reputable foreign correspondents to use the Continental telephone. There would be no more raids on newspaper offices, he assured Mr. BEVERLEY BAXTER, who described the action on Monday night as savouring too much of the Gestapo.

Brass-hats, Captain CAZALET complained, were already getting control, and though it was necessary for them to have a certain amount it must not be forgotten that in a new sense this was a people's war, and the people should be trusted.

Brass-hats were the trouble, not a doubt of it, growled that old campaigner, Colonel WEDGWOOD.

o   o

News from the North
"DECLARATION OF WAR
CREATED PROFOUND IMPRESSION IN
WORKINGTON"
Headings in Local Paper.

REGISTERED

"Name, J. Bull: Occupation, Seeing it Through."

(The National Registration Act creates a National Register [census] and
a system of identity cards. Here John Bull sits in a blacked-out shelter,
prepared to endure the expected air raids.)

"All right, you needn't fly out at me like that – I only said 'Nice if there was an air raid.'"

"We're sitting here drinking tea, and there's a war on."

"I know nothing whatever about that. You see, I have to go to Baden-Baden on account of my health."

"Hi! You mustn't do that – that's 'a fluctuating or warbling signal of varying pitch'!"

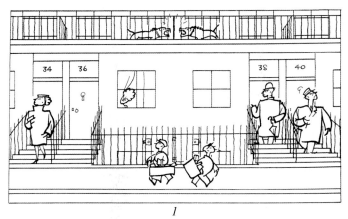

1

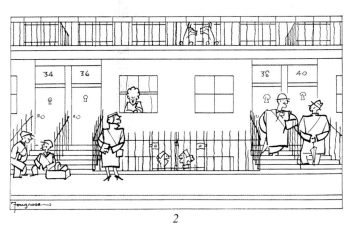

2

THE CHANGING FACE OF BRITAIN.
XVI. – RESIDENTIAL AREA

"Do you think it's some sort of code?"

"I'm sorry, but I'd rather not give an opinion – I think it would really be much better if you yourself choose between them."

Evacuation

With predictions of huge civilian air raid casualties, on September 1, 1939 Operation Pied Piper – the largest mass population movement in British history – began the evacuation of nearly 3 million people out of large cities and towns. Most were schoolchildren, but businesses and government departments were evacuated, too. Over the months of the Phoney War, thousands of children drifted home. But the beginning of air raids in 1940 sent them back to the countryside, a process repeated after each major bombing campaign. For 3.5 million child evacuees, evacuation meant divided families, disrupted education and sometimes worse.

"What I 'ates about this evacuation is the country makes the kids' voices sound so 'ollow."

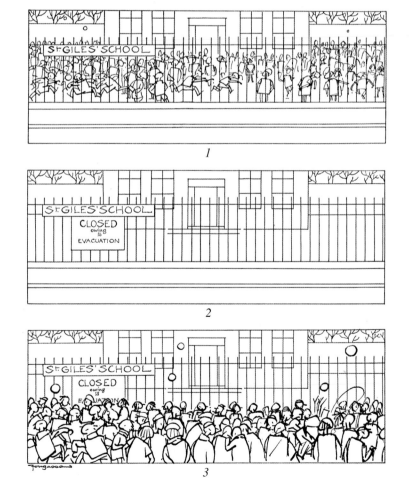

1

2

3

THE CHANGING FACE OF BRITAIN.
XXII. – PRIMARY EDUCATION

"You can tell your teacher you don't want to be evacuated; last time you had it done you had a sore arm for a week, remember."

" Well, for Heaven's sake, don't look in their direction."
" But how can I drive if I don't?"

Mr. PUNCH'S
HOSPITAL COMFORTS FUND

IN A GOOD CAUSE

YOU are asked to think and to think in good time of the wounded. At any moment their needs may become imperative. They will not consider themselves heroes, they will not complain ; they will be those who have neither fallen in action nor come safely through the ordeal, but are part of the reparable human wastage of war ; we shall hear them speaking again—the less seriously disabled — in the language long ago familiar to us : " I got my packet at —— ; I was luckier than some," and yet there will be months of pain in front of them before they can take their place on active service or in civilian life once more.

You are also asked to think of the Navy at sea, the men in the trenches, the men flying, minesweepers, searchlight posts, anti-aircraft stations. All are in exposed, cold, wet situations. They need Balaclava helmets, stockings, socks, mittens and woolly waistcoats for the winter.

Mr. Punch has already bought and distributed :—

Chintz . . .	350	yds.
Bleached Calico .	640	„
Unbleached Calico .	300	„
Turkey Twill . .	50	„
Flannelette . .	3752	„
Winceyette . .	4075	„
Turkish Towelling .	86	„
Ripple Cloth . .	1420	„
Knitting Wool . .	7668	lb.

The buying of this material has absorbed the greater part of the money so far collected, and unless further donations are received the cold winter will be upon us before the comforts can be made up. Every penny subscribed will be used for the comfort of the men serving, or Hospital patients, and no expenses whatever will be deducted. Though we know well that these are days of privation and self-denial for all, we yet ask you, those who can, to send us donations, large or small, according to your means ; for experience in the last war has proved a hundred times over how urgent may be the call and how invaluable is the assistance that can be rendered. Will you please address all contributions and inquiries to :—Punch Hospital Comforts Fund, 10 Bouverie Street, London, E.C.4.

SAFETY FIRST!

LEBENSRAUM

WINGS FROM THE WEST

THE TWO CONSTRICTORS

*"I don't know about helping you, Adolf,
but I do understand your point of view."*

(Hitler and Joachim von Ribbentrop ditch their beliefs, pursuing a
non-aggression pact with Stalin. The war begun, refugees trudge from
the countries Hitler and Stalin have swallowed. Meanwhile, the US arms
embargo lifted, John Bull welcomes armaments from Uncle Sam.)

Gas Masks

Fears that gas attacks would be carried out on Britain's towns and cities were not without foundation. Poison gas had been used on battlefields of the Western Front and more recently against civilians during Mussolini's invasion of Ethiopia. By the outbreak of war in 1939 nearly 38 million gas masks had been issued. Citizens were obliged to carry their masks in their boxy cases at all times, but they soon became a frequently mislaid nuisance. By 1940 scarcely anyone carried their gas masks, even after monthly inspections by air raid wardens began.

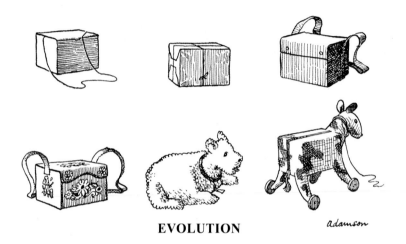

EVOLUTION

"If the government want me to carry my gas-mask, then they ought to make me – it's so utterly ridiculous to leave it to my discretion!"

"Pick it up for us, Sonny. That gas-mask'll be the death o' me."

"I knew I'd hung the darn thing somewhere."

"If this blinkin' rain keeps up much longer we'll 'ave the perishin' Siegfried Line full o' pocket battleships."

"There doesn't seem to be a phrase for 'Your tank is resting on my foot'."

FOLLOW YOUR
TRADE IN THE
FIGHTING
SERVICES

"Please could you make my face a little more military-looking?"

"Don't taste it yet, Sir – they ain't finished messin' abaht wiv it."

"You know, Charlie, this isn't at all the France I expected."

I

II

42

III

IV

The Poet Under Orders

HENCE, loathed melancholy,
    Of A.R.P. and black-out midnight born!
    The Editor desires me to be jolly,
My muse with festive garlands to adorn.
So though the light be dim and irreligious,
    And storied windows blotted everywhere,
We'll greet the sooty gloom with a prodigious
    "WHAT—DO—WE—CARE!"

What do we care if Ribbentrop has been sent to say "Hello!"
To the Esquimaux—
Or if the German High Command have had a kick in the *pantz*
Because they wouldn't agree to submarine bases off the coast of Hants—

Or if Adolf has double-crossed Josef, or pinned on his breast
An Iron Cross, while Josef, visibly impressed,
Whispers in Adolf's ear: "If you've got a nickel,
What about a vodka gorki at the 'Hammer and Sickle'?"
What do we care if the Prime Minister of Zazupittzu
Has replied to the Fuehrer: "Swastikas to you—!"
Or if the Nazis have set up a *"werbegesellschaft"*
On the banks where Charon plies his craft;

Or discovered the First Lord of the Criminality
Guilty of further nautical rascality
And proved beyond doubt that Mr. Chamberlain as a nipper
Worshipped the Borgias and played darts with Jack the Ripper?

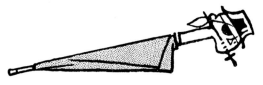

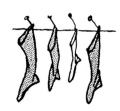

Ladies and, if I may use the abbreviation, gents,
Rid your minds of these grave political events;
They mostly mean that Hitler's knees are knocking—
Hang up your troubles with your Christmas stocking.
(We don't believe that Nazi spies disguised as Nannies
Intend filling the children's stockings with subversive
    pamphlets—that's one of Granny's.)

Besides, the Government is in favour of us popping
Into the shops as usual to do our Christmas shopping.
After all, Aunts Lottie and Pottie must have their handbags,
Even if we can't see the shops for the sandbags.

Talking of sandbags, if yours get homesick, grow mushrooms, or spread diphtheria,
Give them a good dose at bedtime of Jones's *Anti-bagteria*.

So having decided what to give whom—
What about a bottle of "Love in Bloom"
For your little evacuee; and a box
Of Siren Sigars for Grandpa Cox;
And a luminous dog-lead
(Most necessary) for Miss Brede;

And one of those jumpers (*such* a good idea)
Embroidered with our war aims for Alethea;
And a reinforced bowler for Geoff
In the R.A.F.;
And a bag of cement
For dear old Mr. Trent;
And oh! yes, a couple of tins
Of Osoblack for Peterkins?—

Is Your Dog Jittery? PAINT HIM WITH *OSOBLACK*
He'll Think He's Invisible in
Daylight Aerial Attack
Recommended by the N.A.R.P.A.C.
"A perfect *dogsend*," writes Mrs. G.

Having made out your list with care
(And left it heaven knows where),
Join in the Jolly Rush
And the Big Push.
Though you emerge haggard and frayed,
You'll be helping trade—
"And that's the main thing, isn't it, dear Lady Boomery?"
(Blimey! I've left my gas-mask in the "perfumery.")

Outside the Store:
"That voice—that bark—that territorial roar!
Surely we've bumped into each other somewhere before?
Of *course*—it's Colonel Kensington-Gore!"

"This black-out was sure sent to irk us—
Is that you, Someone? Hi! are you there?
Am I in Piccadilly ●
Or am I still in Trafalgar ■ ?"
"Madam, I too am at a loss—
I rather think we're at Charing ✗."

And now as regards
Christmas Cards.
The words this season
Have not only rhyme but reason.

General (A.R.P.) and Mrs. (A.T.S.) Bloodstock-Spear
Wish you a Gamelin Christmas and a Gort New Year.

. . . When the snow lay round about
Deep and crisp and even.
"Snow, my foot!" King Wence called out—
"Them be leaflets, Stephen."

I can't think how the next one got in;
It looks to be of foreign origin.

Poor British Robin in the snow,
There are no crumbs for you, you know ;
Behind that frosted cottage door,
Crumbs feed a family of four.
So we must wish you, Robin dear,
A Hungry Christmas and a Hungrier New Year.

Finally, this is certain to please—
In fact we're sending a lot of these:

May coming joys be larger, sorrows littler ;
A MERRY CHRISTMAS and to ... ... ●.....!

1940

THE DANGEROUS YEAR

"Nearly eight months this war's been on – and what have we got to show for it?"

*"The poor boy's been expecting his 'call-up' any moment
for eight months now."*

*"Good morning, Madam. We're testing gas-
masks – you know, those black rubber things
you had with charcoal containers and straps
that go over the head..."*

FAIRLY HAPPY FAMILIES

(Food rationing is introduced on January 8, 1940. Parodying the game
Happy Families, Minister of Food William Shepherd Morrison, plays
Mr Grits the Grocer.)

"Young gentleman 'ere would like some well-done roast sirloin of beef, new pertaters and cabbidge, and a sweet to foller."

"Poor dear, she lives in constant dread of 'avin' the place knocked down by a bomb – anybody'd think it was 'er own 'ouse!"

"I'll tell nobody where anywhere is."

"It was delivered here months ago – but I really don't know what I'm meant to do with it if the Germans come over."

"Who was that foreign-looking fellow who insisted on seeing the plans?"

"A lady sent me a pair o' socks, Sir, wiv a mouth-organ in one of 'em."

SPRING . . . .

. . . . **RECONNAISSANCE**

" England expects . . ."

Letters to the Secretary of a Golf Club

From Richard Singleton, Club Member, Roughover Golf Club.

DEAR MR. SECRETARY,—Are you aware that when the Germans invaded Holland a great many parachutists were dropped on the golf courses there?

Choice of this particular type of country was deliberate and made for obvious reasons—

(*a*) Excellent cover afforded.

(*b*) Improbability of meeting with human elements—especially military.

(*c*) No telephone-wires, houses or church spires to impede descent.

I suppose you have been asleep (as usual) to the possibilities of their doing the same thing at Roughover.

For heaven's sake wake up.

Yours faithfully,
R. SINGLETON.

PS.—Regarding *cover* (see (*a*) above), one of the first things you ought to do is to fill up all the *deeper* bunkers. As you are well aware, I have for years advocated this (though for other reasons!) especially at the 14th, "Satan's Gullet," and at the 3rd, "Grant's Cavern." Both of these hazards would make admirable places for the concealment of at least a couple of score of the enemy.

From Admiral Charles Sneyring-Stymie, C.B., R.N. (Retd.), The Bents, Rough-over. (Chairman Green Committee.)

DEAR WHELK,—Singleton has been at me about the Germans landing on the links. He is quite right. You *must* take immediate action. Better have all the fairways wired and strewn with impediments; also get the bell at the blind 17th manned by a wideawake squad of caddies so that instant alarm of an impending descent may be given. (Ten sharp clangs with the bell's clapper every thirty seconds ought to do for "public warning" and one clang every ten seconds for "all clear" or "raiders passed.")

I hear Lionel Nutmeg (Malayan Civil Service Retd.) is getting his old elephant gun ready. If you can have this piece of information confirmed, and in the interests of the public's safety, I think you ought to warn the police that he is expected to be at large at any moment.

Yours faithfully,
C. SNEYRING-STYMIE.

From General Sir Armstrong Forcursue, K.B.E., C.S.I. (late Indian Army Retd.), The Cedars, Roughover. (By hand.)

MY DEAR WHELK,—This parachute business can be solved as easily as falling off a log, and believe me, the whole affair only requires a little imagination—and I have got THE VERY THING.

I was talking to Carstairs of the General Outfitters Co., Ltd., in the High Street this morning and he asked me if three old plaster models (Sportsmen's Mannequin Series) complete with lifelike face and adjustable limbs would be of any use to the coming War Supplies Depot's Jumble Sale. Of course when he first mentioned them I asked the man what on earth he took me for; but I have since seen the possibility of their being put to the greatest national use and have just telephoned him to have them left round here at the house as soon as possible.

And now for the plan, which is simplicity itself—*just to dress up the plaster models in some of my old army uniforms and place them in various elevated positions about the links where they can be readily seen from the air.* Reaction on the enemy is obvious, but as you're always so bone dense I'd better explain that the mere fact of three army officers being on duty like *that* will be bound to deter anyone who might be thinking of "dropping off."

So far as our own club members are concerned (and those few of the public who find their way on to the links) I feel quite sure that once they know what the models are there for, and once they get used to them, the whole thing will soon cease to attract attention. I'm afraid, however, that poor old Crookshanks will almost certainly complain that they put him off his game, but you must just be firm with him and tell him there is a war on and he must stretch a point.

As I cannot get the models into position entirely by myself, please come and lend me a hand to dress them up and carry them out on to the course.

Yours sincerely,
ARMSTRONG FORCURSUE.

PS.—To show you how little imagination people have got over this parachute scare—just fancy, that fool Warburtin has bought up every bull-terrier he can lay his hands on in the country. He is training them to go for anything human on sight, with the result that only yesterday one of them took a great hunk out of his wife's shin while she was weeding her herbaceous border. If you ask me, it serves him damn well right.

PPS.—Better come round immediately on receipt of this. Have dinner with us—we can get busy afterwards and put the things out before dusk.

From Mrs. Plantain (wife of Mr. Plantain, Greenkeeper, Roughover Golf Club.) (By Hand.)

SIR,—Please Sir, for goodness sake to come quick for the husband has just taken to his bed owing to what he saw on going out to work at 7 A.M. this morning. And Sir, it is those German parrychooters and they is here all right in our midst, and no mistake, for the husband saw three of them dressed up in old-fashioned British Army uniforms and standing there indifferent like and as if they did not wish to call attention to theirselves. This, he says, was proved by the way one of them was pointing a pair of field-glasses at a clump of whins, another acting he was playing golf, and the third kidding on he was fishing.

Well Sir, for a time the husband just looked his fill, like a rabbit at a weasel and with his heart in his throat, and then Sir he nearly jumped right out of his skin; for suddenly there was a great rushing wind and a lot of swear words just behind him and immediately later there was three loud explosions,

" England expects . . ."

"Where am I?" "I'm afraid we're not allowed to tell you."

and Sir, a moment later *still* the parrychooters was all stone dead.

And it was *that there* club member, Mr. Nutmeg, what is always scowling at everyone, that had bagged the lot—and he did it with the big dangerous gun that he threatened the new groundsman with for not raking the bunkers last summer.

But Sir, what made the husband run home here with the hair on him standing straight up and his lips blue and wanting to blow his nose and to get in quickly under the blankets was *this*—that when the last invader fell over he saw as plain as plain a lot of sawdust and blue smoke and bits of china come out of the dead man's stomach. And, Sir, it was enough to terrify the bravest in the land you must allow.

Well, Mr. Whelk, that is the absolute gospel, for the husband has touched no liquor since the last budget and only a drop then on account of the war-time price, and he is not the one to tell any lies except when provoked by members. So please Sir come quick and bring a doctor with you for he is still sweating something cronic, and I am feared he is in a bad way.

Your obedient Servt.,
ANNIE PLANTAIN.

From General Sir Armstrong Forcursue, K.B.E., C.S.I., The Cedars, Rough-over. (By Hand.)

DEAR WHELK,—Your report received and I have already told the police to have Nutmeg arrested immediately. It is a clear case of sabotage.

Yours faithfully,
ARMSTRONG FORCURSUE.

PS.—Ever since I caught him out telling me he had played eight instead of nine in the 1934 October Club Medal I knew he could never be trusted again. It is amazing we have nursed such a viper in our bosom for so long.

G. C. N.

PUNCH IN WAR-TIME

IN 1914-18 PUNCH was regarded as essential to the Allies' War effort.

Again now it is the endeavour of PUNCH to do everything possible to maintain the good spirits of THE NATION and her ALLIES in the present conflict.

PUNCH is considered a faithful historian and a humorous recorder of the way in which the general public are "carrying on" in War-time. Do not deny yourself the pleasure of its stimulating cartoons, humorous drawings, poems and articles.

UNCONQUERABLE   1914

The Annual Subscription Rate is low: 30/- for addresses in the U.K.; 36/6 Overseas (Canada, 34/-), including all Special and Extra Numbers.

If you are already a regular buyer of PUNCH, you are entitled to specially reduced terms for a Subscription to a member of H.M. or Allied Fighting Forces, and particulars will be gladly sent on application.

All orders and enquiries should be addressed to: The Secretary, PUNCH Offices, 10 Bouverie Street, London, E.C.4.

1940

HOLDING THE BRIDGE

Rationing

With Britain soon to be strangled of imported foods and raw materials, and manufacturing increasingly directed towards the war effort, rationing was inevitable. Food rationing began on January 8, 1940: bacon, butter and eggs were first to go "on the ration". The scheme operated through ration books of coupons that were taken by shopkeepers when goods were bought. With each person allowed a certain amount of rationed items per week, the authorities tried to ensure everyone had their fair share. Petrol, rationed from 1939, ceased to be available to private motorists in June 1942, while clothing was rationed from June 1941. Though many items – like bread – were never rationed, there were frequent shortages.

"I come, Effendi, to gratify thy every wish – with the exception, of course, of meat, sugar, butter and petrol."

"Of course the reason that we've got so much is that none of us care for sugar."

"I can't move on – I've used up all my units."

Impressions of Parliament

Whit Monday, May 13th.—Meeting briefly, both Houses gave the new Administration a stirring reception. In both the motion was the same: "That this House welcomes the formation of a Government representing the united and inflexible resolve of the nation to prosecute the war with Germany to a victorious conclusion." In the Lords it was passed unanimously, and the division forced on the Commons by the preposterous attitude of Mr. MAXTON and Mr. STEPHEN resulted in figures of 381 votes to nil—both these recalcitrant and perverse gentlemen having to act as tellers, who score nothing for their side.

Lord HALIFAX's reference to Mr. CHAMBERLAIN's disinterested public spirit brought cheers, the loudness of which were only matched by his estimation of the value to the country of the new P.M.'s imagination, daring, and determination. The attack which had been launched on the Belgian and Dutch peoples without warning and in defiance of scrupulously observed neutrality, said the FOREIGN SECRETARY, gave the measure of lawless savagery which it was now the duty of civilised nations to stamp out. The Germans had been uniformly treacherous. The new Government of all the parties was our immediate answer. Lord SNELL declared that we had pooled all our strength in order to restore decency on earth, and Lord CREWE, the PRIMATE and others warmly supported the resolution.

Mr. CHURCHILL got an immense ovation from the Commons, and having said that he hoped soon to complete his appointments and apologised for the lack of ceremony with which in the emergency he had had to reform the Government, he said: "I would say to the House as I said to those who have joined this Government: 'I have nothing to offer but blood, toil, tears and sweat.' We have before us an ordeal of the most grievous kind. We have before us many, many long months of struggle and of suffering. You ask what is our policy. I will say: 'It is to wage war by sea, land and air with all our might and with all the strength that God can give us, and to wage war against a monstrous tyranny,

AT THE HELM
THE PRIME MINISTER

never surpassed in the dark, lamentable catalogue of human crime.' That is our policy. You ask what is our aim. I can answer in one word: It is victory, victory at all costs, victory in spite of all terrors, victory, however long and hard the road may be, for without victory there is no survival—let that be realised—no survival for the British Empire, no survival for all that the British Empire has stood for no survival for the urge and impulse of the ages, that mankind will move forwards towards its goal. I take up my task with buoyancy and hope, and I feel sure that our cause will not be suffered to fail among men. At this time I feel entitled to claim the aid of all, and I say: 'Come, then, let us go forward with our united strength.'"

Words chosen so perfectly left little else to be said. Mr. LEES-SMITH told the House how overwhelmingly the Labour Conference had backed the decision of the party leaders to join the Government. Sir PERCY HARRIS entirely approved of the coalition movement, though he hoped the House would continue to function as a constructive critic. Mr. LLOYD GEORGE congratulated jointly the country and Mr. CHURCHILL, who he said had been called at a graver moment than had ever confronted a British Prime Minister. Mr. MAXTON, so often wise Mr. MAXTON, so often witty Mr. MAXTON, talked a good deal of unrealistic nonsense. Moved not by him but by a remembrance that history at that moment was unrolling yet another of her bloody canvases not very far away, the House broke up. Until, barring emergencies, May 21st.

"NOW ALL ARE FOR THE STATE"

R.A.F., SIR ARCHIBALD SINCLAIR (Lib.); ARMY, MR. EDEN (Cons.);
NAVY, MR. ALEXANDER (Lab.)

LITTLE ADOLF HEAD-IN-AIR

(Parodying the children's story *Struwwelpeter*, Adolf Hitler is about to
come a cropper with his plans to invade Britain.)

"I heard a rumour that Lord Haw Haw has given the inside story about Mrs. Robinson and the Women's Institute Prize Cake Competition."

WAR-TIME WEAKNESSES – SEEING SPIES

"Yes, sir, I am aware that the posters say 'Freedom is in peril, defend it with all your might' – nevertheless, I'm afraid I can't let you pass along here without a permit."

"Stop, dear, stop! – John's been posted to the Middle East."

When one looks around one, one has to admit that not every change brought about by the war—

—has been for the worse.

THE CHANGING FACE OF BRITAIN AGAIN

"I'm beginning to wish we'd commandeered somewhere else for Divisional Headquarters."

"A thousand pounds' worth of three per-cent. National Defence Bonds and a three-ha'penny stamp, please."

"Gosh! I wonder what you would all have found to talk about if there hadn't been any war."

*" But you must remember that I outnumbered
them by one to three."*

*"Cigarettes, boys? These are herbal and
home-made!"*

"Quick – follow that Heinkel!"

*"Eglantine Cottage? Go down the lane past the Messerschmitt, bear left and keep
on past the two Dorniers, then turn sharp right and it's just past the first Junkers."*

THE LITTLE SHIPS SAIL ON.

(Watched by the ghost of Sir Francis Drake, one of the Little Ships of the
Dunkirk Evacuation sails into legend.)

The Big Push

FOR weeks I had been saying to myself "I must look in at the Wilhelmstrasse and see how they are all getting on," but I kept putting it off. Then, in last Sunday's paper, I read that article by Mme. Tabouis. "Germany," she said, "is in the throes of a chaotic military muddle. Each group is torn by dissension." I grabbed my hat and hurried round. I saw that I had been missing something good.

"Is the Fuehrer in?" I asked of the genial storm-trooper at the door.

"Not yet, Sir," he replied. "But the conference is called for eleven. Go right in. You will find all the boys there."

The front office was full, as any room would be that contained Field-Marshal Goering. I noticed several groups, all torn by dissension. I joined a couple of Generals who were chatting in low voices by the umbrella-stand.

"Don't seem to get us anywhere, these conferences," one was saying. "Just a waste of time."

"It's those bright ideas of our beloved Leader's that hang things up," assented the other. "I do sometimes wish he would leave military affairs to the military."

At this moment the umbrella-stand moved from its place and arrested the two speakers. The Gestapo never sleeps and Himmler is a master of disguise. A few minutes later the Fuehrer bustled in.

"Well, here we all are," he said. "Now, about getting this war started. Anybody any suggestions?"

"I was thinking——" said Ribbentrop.

"What with?" said Goering, who has a great gift for repartee.

"Now, boys, boys," said the Fuehrer indulgently. "Cut out the cracks. We're all working for the good of the show. Here's a thought that crossed my mind as I was coming here. Let's destroy Britain."

"Er—how?" asked Party Member Hess.

"Invade her, of course. Yes, yes, I know we haven't guaranteed her neutrality, but one's got to do the irregular thing sometimes. Our troops cross the North Sea, escorted by pocket battleships. You did say," he added, turning to Goebbels, "that we had destroyed the British Fleet?"

"Well," said the Doctor, a little embarrassed, "we have sunk the *Ark Royal* seven times, but——"

"Oh, all right, then. Let's wait till the North Sea freezes, and skate across."

"The North Sea does not freeze."

"Why not? The Baltic does."

"In the case of the North Sea, there would appear to be some local rule."

"Oh? Well, then, let's destroy France."

There was an awkward silence.

"One is faced with certain difficulties, Leader," said General Brauchitsch, with an embarrassed cough. "The Maginot Line——"

"What's that?"

"Well, Leader, it's a little difficult to describe exactly. It consists of— how shall I put it?— a number of fortified positions——"

"Why wasn't I told about this Maginot Line? Don't I get any co-operation?"

"And then of course," said Ribbentrop, "we are rather trying to conciliate France. But I don't understand the French. We go out of our way to entertain them with excellent lectures on the loud-speaker, and they shoot off

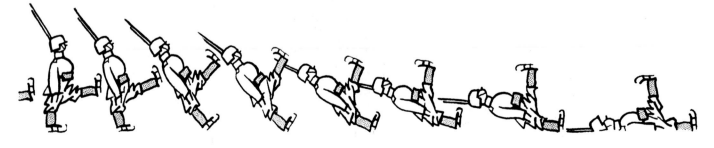

machine-guns at us. The other day we actually went to the expense of engaging a brass band——"

The Fuehrer held up his hand.

"Don't say any more. I've got it. My secret weapon. German bands. There was a time when they were the scourge of England. Read the English national poet, Calverley. Look through the back numbers of *Punch*. It is the one thing England dreads. We attack by air. A hundred thousand parachutes, each dropping a man with a trombone. They land and form units. Well, look, boys, work it out for yourselves. Imagine Churchill trying to concentrate, with a couple of German bands—one playing Verdi and the other Wagner—outside his window. And the same all over London. To get a German band to go away you have to give them a shilling. How long could the finances of any nation stand the drain of constantly paying out shillings? Within a year the country will be bled white."

Field - Marshal Goering glanced round the gathering. His eyes were gleaming.

"Nice work, Leader," he said. "I think, gentlemen, that I shall not be misinterpreting the sentiments of this meeting if I say 'Heil Hitler!'"

"Heil Hitler!" came the crashing chorus.

"Against this secret weapon of our Leader's the British have no defence."

"Suppose they suck lemons?" said a musical voice. I recognised it as that of Mme. Tabouis, and was surprised, for I had not known that she was present, though she generally is. Then I saw that an aspidistra across the room was quivering gently.

The Fuehrer looked about him, frowning. He was obviously in one of his pets.

"Who said that?"

"It sounded like Goering," said Ribbentrop.

"I thought it was Ribbentrop," said Goering.

"There's something in it, you know," said Brauchitsch thoughtfully. "It would wreck the whole thing."

"So now we've got to start all over again," said the Fuehrer fretfully. He paused a moment. "Look, how would this be? Bore a tunnel under France and Spain and come up alongside Gibraltar."

I left them at it, and went round the corner for a blotting-paper sandwich and a cup of blackberry coffee.

P. G. W.

To a Favourite Barrage Balloon

GOLD in the dawn I've seen you shine,
    And silver in the moon,
Cherished your beauty, called you mine—
O more than a Balloon!

For me what varying spells you weave!—
    Now white against the blue,
Now dark against a stormy eve,
    So changeable, yet true.

Serene, ethereal, free you ride;
    They say you are, I know,
To some invisible anchor tied,
    But yet it seems not so;

Rather it is as though borne high
    By pure inviolate will
You hold your station in the sky
    To bid me comfort still.

* * * * *

To-day I walked through (Hush-hush) Square,
    Where oft my footsteps pass,
And dun and dingy you were there,
    Lurching upon the grass.

Penned within privets, planes and rails
    On lawns of sooty green,
With cylinders and huts and pails,
    Looking—no, not obscene—

But conjuring up a mixture, say,
    Of whale, deflated frog,
Hot-water-bottle in decay:
    A dismal catalogue.

'Twas ever thus. Stay! I would not
    Be fickle like the rest:
Should auld acquaintance be forgot?
    The heart within my breast

Bids me deny that cynic scorn,
    Bids me ignore my pain,
For on some blissful future morn
    They'll blow you up again.

Once more you'll sail the untrodden
        ways
    Our London's streets above,
And I shall still be there to praise
    And (*faute de mieux*) to love.   J. C. S.

"Then I can definitely count on you next Saturday to make a fourth for digging tank-traps?"

"What I said was, 'My husband is leaving on a frantically hush-hush mission to Belgrade on Tuesday!'"

"These war-time batteries are so frightfully weak!"

"The trouble is that every day I'm finding it increasingly difficult to remain a Defeatist."

"Of course in the normal way the horizon would be covered with hundreds of advancing enemy troops and the sky black with countless dive-bombers."

"Remember – when I write 'Love to Aunt Maggie,' it means 'The grub's awful and Sergeant's been giving me hell.'"

P. G. W.

The next issue of *Punch* will contain a hitherto unpublished story by Mr. P. G. Wodehouse entitled *The Word in Season*. It was sent to us not long before the Channel coast was occupied by the German armies; and Mr. Wodehouse, who was living at Touquet, still retains, we understand, possession of his house, and is as comfortable as the trying circumstances make possible.

"Three hundred and seventy-six, three hundred and seventy-seven, three hundred and seventy-eight. Swastikas as plain as pikestaffs."

THICKER THAN WATER

"Now, Sam, step on it!"

(With France about to fall, Franklin Roosevelt tries to persuade
an isolationist US Congress to increase the flow of munitions and
equipment to the Allies.)

READING THE SKIES

"I have conquered all Gaul. How long will it take to conquer all Britain?" "Wait a moment, Leader, while I look at the omens of the air."

THE GREAT PROTECTOR

THE HOUR OF THE HYENA

SAVE FOR THE BRAVE

(Cast as Caesar, Hitler asks soothsayer Joseph Goebbels for his predictions on the invasion of Britain. A menacing Hermann Goering confiscates all property in Poland, a prowling Mussolini marks Italy's declaration of war on June 10, while the War Savings Campaign reached a total of £100 million and 60,000 "Savings Groups".)

A·R·P

ARP, the acronym for Air Raid Precautions, came to be attached to the volunteers of the Air Raid Wardens Service who wore the initials emblazoned across their steel helmets. Though much mocked for their officious enforcement of blackout regulations, they played a vital role during air raids, touring their sector as bombs fell, directing people to air raid shelters and reporting incidents. The ARP were often first on the scene in the aftermath of a raid, helping casualties and coordinating the emergency response.

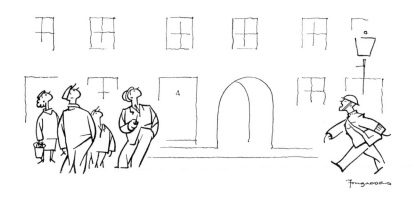

"Now then pass along there, please – the 'All-Clear's' gone, and absolutely nothing more to be seen."

"Good evening, Madam. Over nine months ago – on the 3rd of September, 1939, to be precise – we declared war on Germany."

"You can't report you THINK *an unexploded bomb fell in here. You must search the place."*

WATCHERS OF THE SEA

(On June 13 the ringing of church bells was banned. Now they were
to sound only as a signal of Britain being invaded. Here a group of
countrymen, among them John Bull, keep watch on the English Channel.)

THE ROCK AND THE STORM

(Hermann Goering, supreme commander of the Luftwaffe, is the face of
the storm that batters Britain as Germany tries to achieve mastery of the
air so that Hitler's invasion can take place.)

"...meanwhile, in Britain, the entire population, faced by the threat of invasion, has been flung into a state of complete panic..."

"Todbury, Sir? Oh, yes, Sir. You want to turn round and go straight back for twelve miles."

"Furthermore it is essential that all personnel should be impressed with the immediate probability of large-scale air-raids – and this is especially necessary when there is no immediate probability of large-scale air-raids."

HOME THOUGHTS FROM ABROAD

Impressions of Parliament

Business Done

Tuesday, September 17th. — House of Lords: Statement on the War by Lord Caldecote. Secret Session on Future Parliamentary Arrangements.

House of Commons: War Statement by Mr. Winston Churchill. Secret Session on Arrangements.

Wednesday, September 18th. — House of Lords: Discussion on British Propaganda Abroad. Secret Session on Air Raids.

House of Commons: Secret Session on Air Raids.

Thursday, September 19th. — House of Commons: Secret Session on Air Raids (continued).

Tuesday, September 17th. — It is, doubtless, appropriate that a democratically-elected body like the House of Commons should look somewhat shamefaced when it goes into secret session. And that certainly accounts for the rosy blush that suffused the face of the PRIME MINISTER when, apparently in the middle of a speech, he "spied strangers" and drove from the Chamber even your humble scribe.

As a matter of record it was his second blush of the day. Of the other, more anon.

THE OLD LADY WHOSE FLESH CREEPS

"Newspaper people give me a sort of creepy feeling." — *Lord Addison.*

In the Lords the same procedure was being followed at the behest of Lord CALDECOTE, who *never* blushes. Before the impenetrable veil of secrecy descended, his Lordship proudly told the Upper House that he had heard no complaints about the conditions in which we were all living and working. In London, in a week, rescue parties had turned out 169 times and had saved 216 lives.

The Archbishop of CANTERBURY, whose age-old traditional home is in the midst of one of the hard-hit areas, was given a sympathetic cheer as he told how 200 bereaved men, women and children were nightly seeking the sanctuary of his chapel crypt against the pagan attackers from the air.

Mr. CHURCHILL'S first blush of the day — a good healthy ruddy one it was too — came when Mr. A. V. ALEXANDER, First Lord of the Admiralty, announced the renaming of the destroyers made over to us by the United States Government. Mr. ALEXANDER openly hero-worships the P.M., and it was with a considerable flourish that he announced: "The Leader — CHURCHILL."

What used to be called loud and prolonged cheers. The original owner of the name slid down in his seat, head on chest, to cover his embarrassment, but in response to cries he "held his head up" — to reveal an ear-to-ear grin as well as the blush.

The other destroyers are to be called: *Caldwell, Cameron, Castleton, Chelsea, Chesterfield, Clare* and *Campbeltown.* All are of towns common to both Britain and the United States.

In his war statement Mr. CHURCHILL remarked, a thought wistfully, that the state of being keyed up to highest pitch day after day had lost its first charm of novelty. He might have added that the wail of the sirens, just then floating in through the windows, had also lost that endearing quality.

Those very windows, by the way, had a novelty of their own, for the familiar stained glass had given way to plain, rather dusty-looking, glass. The hidden lighting in the roof stood out naked and glaring, for the glass screen had also gone to a place of greater security.

The PRIME MINISTER found in the R.A.F.'s destruction of 185 German warplanes in a single day (Sunday, September 15th) "reason for sober and increasing confidence." The main German attacks on London were in the hope of terrorizing the inhabitants into submission and into pressing the Government to make peace.

Mr. CHURCHILL'S massive jaw stuck out as he declared sturdily that the ruse would not succeed. A roar of cheers confirmed his view.

Another big mistake Messrs. HITLER, GOERING, RIBBENTROP and Company had made was the attack on "our beloved KING and QUEEN" — Buckingham Palace had been bombed three times in as many days. This attack

"THE DESTROYERS"

"The strength of twice three thousand horse
That serve the one command."
Kipling.

THE FIRST LORD OF THE ADMIRALTY

only united the Royal Family more closely with the nation in new and sacred bonds.

"And," the Premier added, his chin jutting out again, "this will increase our determination to carry on an unrelenting prosecution of the war against so foul a foe!"

Just *how* foul a foe he proceeded to elaborate by announcing that, in a fortnight, the gallant *Luftwaffe* had killed 2,000 civilians and injured another 8,000, while the casualties in the fighting forces had been a mere 250. Even these bitter blows, however, had not made any serious difference to our war effort. And we were making "grievous inroads" on the German air superiority.

So far, a sombre, even macabre, statement. But the PRIME MINISTER cannot make a speech entirely devoid of the lighter touch. He coined the name "Jim Crows" for the new roof-top watchers against air-raids.

Then — "casting his eye around," he spied strangers.

The Attorney-General (Sir DONALD SOMERVELL), with a fine sense of the dramatic and perhaps an unnecessary warning to the Fourth Estate, asked

"Curse it! Missed the Grand Slam!"

for and got leave for the Clerk of the House to give evidence in a police court against someone alleged to have spilled the beans about an earlier secret session.

Wednesday, September 18th.—Their Lordships heard Lord ADDISON urge that more should be made abroad of the British case by means of better propaganda. He made the now seemingly inevitable suggestion that Lord BEAVERBROOK should become Minister of Propaganda. Newspapermen, said Lord ADDISON, with an uneasy sidelong glance at the Press Gallery, always gave him a creepy feeling—perhaps because he knew nothing of their world. But when it came to presenting a case to the best advantage they were the people to do the trick.

Lord SIMON, rising from the Woolsack, promised to convey to "the proper quarter" the suggestion about the future of Lord BEAVERBROOK. Presumably to Lord BEAVERBROOK?

Mr. ATTLEE, whose rather professorial manner riles the House with curious consistency, was in trouble in the Commons about a committee of Civil Servants and Service chiefs who select recipients of war honours and decorations. It was not so much what he said, apparently, as the "nasty way he said it." However, he survived to move (without the slightest sign of a blush) a second secret session, this time about raids, shelters, feeding and whatnot.

Thursday, September 19th.—There was a big cheer when Mr. NEVILLE CHAMBERLAIN, fresh back from illness, made his appearance in the Commons. He bowed his acknowledgments to both sides of the House.

Sir JOHN ANDERSON, normally the most urbane of Ministers, showed a new snappiness in reply to questioners. He said there were 750,000 files relating to aliens, and expressed the view that an occasional mislaying of one of them was not a matter for intense astonishment.

Mr. ATTLEE got into another minor *blitzkrieg*, this time because he was judged to have snorted at a suggestion that the PRIME MINISTER's big speeches should be broadcast.

Pertinacious Mr. GEOFFREY MANDER wanted the Government to make biscuits as an iron ration for civilians, but the idea did not seem to go down very well, especially as some of the M.P.s had missed their early meals through the activities of the King's enemies.

Mr. ATTLEE having moved the customary motion resolving the House into secret session, everybody went out, just as Mr. WILL THORNE was complaining to Mr. ROBERT BOOTHBY, of the Food Ministry, that he had been unable to get "even a small glass of milk." We shall never know how that earth-shaking problem was solved—or even if it was.

o　　o

"Australian black swans are among the birds that do well at Whipsnade Zoo . . . One pair this year brought off a brood of three goslings."—*Evening News.*

A divorce is anticipated.

The Blitz

British cities and towns endured air raids from August 1940 until the last pilotless V-rocket fell in March 1945. But the Blitz – the sustained Luftwaffe bombing campaign between September 1940 and May 1941 – has passed into legend. While garden-owning suburbanites, like the couple below, could use Anderson shelters, initially there were few public shelters for inner city residents. Many Londoners felt safest in Underground stations, despite the misgivings of the government. It soon realised the benefits of using the Tube and introduced facilities for the sheltering crowds. The cage-like Morrison Shelters (p.121) were introduced in March 1941.

"In any case you're well over the white line."

"...and here is another bit of news which has just come through."

"There you are, it's what I've always said – anyone who had been sitting on the mantelpiece would have been perfectly safe."

"It's no use getting fed up and wanting to go back to the house, John. The first night we don't sleep in the shelter there's certain to be an air raid!"

"*Well, I suppose you've guessed. I'm called to the Colours.*"

THE FRONT LINE

THE LIGHTS O' LONDON
OR HAPPY DREAMS

*"...so I want you all to become even more
potato-minded than usual."*

"Just there. 15/-, whole head perm."

*"What's an easy type of Jerry plane to
start on, Sergeant?"*

First hour,

Second hour.

Third hour.

Fourth and following hours.

WAR'S HUMANIZING INFLUENCE.
THE SHELTER TRENCH.

"I wonder what our brave sailors who bring them to us would say if they knew that out of a dozen of your foreign eggs two were bad!"

"You should have laid more stress on the fact that we were business evacuees."

"I'm so sorry, young man. I'd no idea we'd strayed into a military zone."

"It's all right; it's all right.
It's only an air-raid!"

"We're going on to the next station; it's a better programme."

"Don't stand there knocking, Roberts, go straight in."

HIS USUAL SEAT

PUNCH

OR
THE LONDON CHARIVARI

Vol. CXCIX   No. 5194   October 9 1940

Charivaria

"DURING the last war Herr HITLER tried to save the life of a drowning Italian," says the *Giornale d'Italia*. Still, he's done far worse things than that since then.

o   o

Moments in Bloomsbury

"Riley sat at the back, with Miss Blandish lying on his feet, biting his nails."—*Extract from novel of the hour*.

o   o

"Can you picture Marshal GOERING striding along a quiet English lane?" asks an imaginative correspondent. No. What are tank-traps for?

o   o

It is rumoured that the reapers of Germany never speak to each other. They remember that corn has ears.

o   o

Restoring Calm

"There was still a good deal of loud talk, which only subsided with Bailie Keane calling for members of the Sewerage and Slaughter-house Committee to remain behind for a meeting."—*Scottish Paper*.

o   o

The War Office has idiotically declined our suggestion of a baboon barrage over Regent's Park on the grounds that it would be only suitable for gorilla warfare.

A radio critic points out that a home-made condenser, costing only sixpence, will make an effective silencer for a noisy wireless-set. So will a sledge-hammer or even a hatchet.

o   o

"A fire was started, but was quickly subdued, and the only damage to exhibits was in a part of the Museum set aside for members of the staff."—*Daily Sketch*.

And who cares about them?

o   o

A Militiaman's mother writing in a daily paper says that since her son has been in camp his cheeks have grown much rounder. Apparently he is a bugler.

o   o

Many of the B.B.C. staff sleep in the Concert Hall. This recital is never broadcast.

o   o

We understand that the small field in the Eastern Counties, in which no German plane has yet crashed, is to be thrown open shortly to sightseers in aid of the Spitfire Fund.

o   o

HITLER is said to dislike oysters and always ignores them at a banquet. Perhaps that explains it—he is waiting until there isn't an *r* in the month.

THE

COMBAT

" I don't mind putting my car out of action every night, but having to make it go again every morning is going to drive me mad!"

CONVERSATION PIECE

"Give him my compliments and tell him that, while we admire the subtlety of his point, we prefer to assume that the black-out regulations do NOT apply to searchlights."

*"So our poor old Empire is alone in the world." "Aye, we are
– the whole five hundred million of us."*

*"Morning Miss Twigg, yes I am still alive then and
they were right over our house too, where's the
correspondence?"*

"Why, them Germans is that dirty they even drop bombs on you after the 'All-Clear''s gorn."

1941
Friends and Allies

"It's the military – asking if they can commandeer the house."

"Air-raid message white received."

"Lucky? I'll say we were lucky!"

THE DRAGON-SLAYER

"So much for that one, and now to face the next."

"A pump and crew must be standing by day and night, fully equipped and ready to leave at a moment's notice. We never know when we may be called out on a regional exercise."

"Look, dear, a contract from ENSA!"

"Pore lil' feller – I told Emily when she went into munitions that he'd never make a shopper."

WAR-TIME WEAKNESSES – PREOCCUPATION

The Home Guard

By May 1940 the German Army neared the English Channel and it seemed that Britain would soon face invasion. Private home defence groups began forming – to the alarm of the government which thought fighting best left to the military. Under pressure, on May 13, it announced the formation of the Local Defence Volunteers (LDV). Within a week 250,000 had volunteered. In July 1940 the LDV were renamed the Home Guard, on the insistence of Churchill himself. At first uniformed with an armband and armed with pitchforks and shotguns, it became better equipped as the war went on.

"I've laid your uniform out, my Lord."

"Yes, he's at our secret observation post. Follow the wire."

"Yes, I can come and 'elp with the garden reg'lar every Friday, but there's one thing, Mum, if the invasion should come on a Friday I shouldn't be able to come that day as I'm in the 'Ome Guard."

"This comes of listening to all that talk about the Napoleonic wars."

BIG FIRE CHIEF

" Then felt I like some watcher of the skies. . . ."

(With compulsory firewatching imposed on January 20, Home Secretary
Herbert Morrison is shown in full firewatcher's gear.)

Firewatching

The destructive potential of incendiary bombs came to the fore after the catastrophic raid on the City of London over the night of Sunday, December 29, 1940 when St Paul's Cathedral was almost destroyed. With business premises unoccupied, fires quickly took hold and a lethal firestorm ensued. St Paul's survived through the efforts of its volunteer firewatchers and the Fire Service – instructed by Churchill to save the iconic structure at all costs. On January 20, 1941 the firewatching of unoccupied business premises became compulsory. The small stick-like incendiaries could be extinguished effectively by the easily-used stirrup pump.

"Splendid! Splendid! You've ALMOST got the hang of it."

"Wake up, old chap, time for you to go off duty."

"Actually this is very much as Wren INTENDED us to see St. Paul's."

"Blast these air-raid warnings! It's only about eight hours since the last one."

"Would you mind paying attention, Mrs Eglethorpe, please? I hope you don't think they enclose directions with the bomb."

"Oh, Mr Butterfield, Mr Fitzsimmons would like to see you in his office at once."

Uncle Frederic at 8.32 p.m. last Thursday – if his description is strictly in accordance with the facts.

"I only got your letter posted just in time. Next minute the pillar-box disappeared."

"One can only presume that, for some reason, the Germans considered it was worth preserving."

Impressions of Parliament

Business Done

Tuesday, May 20th.—House of Lords: Their Lordships Get a Surprise.

House of Commons: The Premier Tells of the Attack on Crete; Fire Services Bill, all stages.

Tuesday, May 20th.—The House of Commons was in one of its "moods" to-day. And so, for that matter, was the House of Lords—but of that more anon.

Question-time can be a demi-Paradise for Ministers. Or it can be a demi-Other Place. To-day was one of those snappy days, with incipient "scenes" over all sorts of queer and (normally) unconsidered trifles, and the mildest of men hurling themselves into rages.

Captain A. M. LYONS, for instance, normally a model of old-world courtesy, had a regular up-and-downer with (you

IN TRAINING

"Proposals for improving the distribution of eggs are in an advanced stage of preparation."—*Major LLOYD GEORGE, Parliamentary Secretary to the Ministry of Food.*

will never guess!) even-gentler Major LLOYD GEORGE. It began with a question about profiteering in tinned marmalade, and the Captain ended the row with the announcement that he would raise a debate later.

Then Sir JOHN WARDLAW-MILNE acidly pointed out to the Home Office that it was "very difficult for a man to answer a charge that had not been made." Which seemed reasonable enough, but it was the way he said it.

Miss ELEANOR RATHBONE, not to be outdone, complained about property-owners who made *no arrangements* for fire-watching their premises—"and are not there to see that they are executed." Dr. LITTLE, from Ireland, looked enviously at this poacher of bulls.

Mr. HAROLD MACMILLAN, of the Supply Ministry, averted another attempted blitz by assuring the House that the PRIME MINISTER (who sat, mask-faced, on the Treasury Bench) was "never wholly satisfied with Supply; his position is one of qualified optimism."

Captain DAVID MARGESSON, War Minister, scored the nearest approach to a success with an announcement that the uniform allowance for new officers is to be £35, instead of £30. But even this led to a demand from Mr. BELLENGER for its back-dating to the beginning of the war—or it might have been the beginning of the Army; it is hard to hear Mr. BELLENGER at the end of a sentence. The concession will date from January 1st last.

Mr. HAROLD NICOLSON, of the Ministry of Information, cheered the House up a little by expressing the view that publication of news of bombing of some famous buildings (to wit, the Houses of Parliament), and withholding it in other cases, was "not Government policy, but common-sense."

Major VYVYAN ADAMS, whose humour is of the corrosive type, chose as his victim not one of our own Ministers, but Herr RUDOLF HESS, Minister to none other than Der Fuehrer of Germany. This gentleman, now visiting Britain after an adventurous flight and parachute descent, the Major described as a "bloodstained crook," adding a word of condemnation of those who indulged in "nauseating rhapsodies" on HESS's personality.

Mr. CHURCHILL (with, it seemed, an envious glance at one who could employ such richness of imagery) replied that he would not do anything to detract from its flowery elegance, whereupon the Major threw in a complaint that *The Times* had called "this creature" an idealist.

Mr. GEORGE HICKS, of the Ministry of Works and Buildings, is a Trade Union leader who is not used to being answered back, and, challenged about payments by an outside body to an official of his Department, got very involved on the subject of "principle." Payment to an official of £1 was as bad—or as good—as £10,000 if the principle were wrong, said he, and £10,000 was as good—or as bad—as £1 if the principle were right.

The HOME SECRETARY's Bill authorizing the Nationalization of all Fire Brigades was carried through all its stages in one day.

The House looked embarrassed by this out-of-order disquisition on ethics and morals, which reached its end just in time to save its author from rebuke by Mr. SPEAKER.

Mr. CHURCHILL, as so often before, restored unity to the House by rising and, without a single note, giving a swift review of the war's recent developments.

We had captured Amba Alagi, in Abyssinia, with the Duke of AOSTA, the Italian Commander-in-Chief. This marked the end of organized resistance in the land of the Negus, already happily restored to his throne in Addis Ababa. Our campaign had been one of the most remarkable ever waged by British or Imperial troops, and was months ahead of schedule. The South African Army and, above all, the Indian Army, had played memorable parts in the battles, winning the honour and admiration of their British comrades.

Then he broke the news about the sudden air-borne attack by the Germans on Crete, seat of the Greek Government. We had continually bombed German concentrations of aircraft in Southern Greece, but this had not prevented the arrival of a good many in Crete. There would be stern resistance from the British, New Zealand and Greek Forces on the island, fighting under General FREYBERG, V.C.

Later in the day, Mr. CHURCHILL added that the battle was developing rapidly, and that the Germans had landed 1,500 troops in New Zealand battle-dress—an exposure that was greeted by cries of "Shame!" from all over the House.

PORTENT IN AFRICA

[According to Reuter, great rejoicing has been caused in Somaliland by the appearance of a magnificent new comet.]

(By February 1941 General Archibald Wavell, Commander-in-Chief
Middle-East Command, was achieving success against Italian forces in
Libya, Eritrea and Ethiopia.)

1. – Good news

2. – Not quite so good news

3. – Worse news

4. – Definitely worse news

5. – Still worse news

6. – Bad news

THE CHANGING FACE OF BRITAIN.

XXXIV. – News

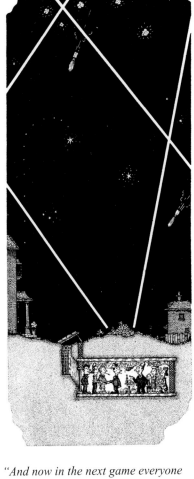

"And now in the next game everyone goes outside except me."

WAR-TIME WEAKNESSES – ASKING SILLY QUESTIONS

"It's gone to old Brown's head a little – catching the first chink of the season."

"I think I ought to use this stamp again, it's hardly marked."

PUNCH

OR
THE LONDON CHARIVARI

Vol. CC   No. 5233

June 25 1941

Charivaria

ACCORDING to an Ankara news message those 1,700 German air force officers and specialists who were not in Syria have now arrived back in Germany.

o   o

We read of a Vienna girl who was sent to prison for trying to pull out a handful of Dr. GOEBBELS' hair. Perhaps she wanted to put it in a locket.

o   o

A gossip-writer observes that the lettuce he planted turned out to be radish. Which of course isn't at all bad for an amateur.

o   o

A Yorkshire clergyman announces his retirement from rugby football. Opponents who met him on the field will never forget his severe clerical collar.

o   o

Now You Know

"London, April 13 (Canadian Press)—The British Broadcasting Corporation reported today that the Maharaja of Jodhpur has received a commission as a second lieutenant in the Life Guards [the British service similar to the United States Coast Guard]."
American Paper.

o   o

A London restaurant advertises that it has no music, homely cooking, quiet, efficient service and an old-time atmosphere. What! *Onions?*

Before the war Germany dumped thousands of cheap alarm clocks in this country. Which is probably why we took such a long time to wake up.

o   o

An American newspaper man says he once interviewed GOEBBELS in his office and noticed a picture of HITLER on the wall. What did he expect? A picture of GEORGE WASHINGTON?

o   o

Cutting the Cackle

"The wedding was a quiet one, there being no bridesmaids."
Yorkshire Paper.

o   o

"Men's hats are obtainable without coupons and may actually become cheaper," we are told. This news has caused grim smiles on the saturnine faces of hotel cloak-room brigands.

o   o

The new Abyssinian coinage now being minted in this country has, we are told, a hole stamped in the middle. MUSSOLINI, of course, made a hole in most of the previous issue.

o   o

We are told that if the Germans invade this country they must be delayed as much as possible and kept away from the railway. This sounds contradictory.

D D

105

Dig for Victory

Britain imported around 55 million tons of food a year as the war began. Now merchant ships were under attack from U-boats and better used to help with the war effort. Aware of impending shortages and anxious that people had a healthy diet, in October 1939 the Ministry of Agriculture launched the *Dig for Victory* campaign urging citizens to grow their own food. The campaign was hugely successful, especially after Lord Woolton was appointed Minister of Food, and allotments sprouted in unlikely places. Apart from vegetables, people were encouraged to keep a few chickens for eggs – and even goats and rabbits.

"...and this war will be won on the turnip-fields of Little Muggleton."

"Can you think of anything else we used not to be able to keep in this district?"

"So you see, dear, one can *be* decorative *and* useful.*"

"They make fun of her now, but she stopped the invasion in June."

Home Guard Goings-On

A Jerk in It

IN the past, except for a number of uplifting pamphlets and a single thrilling glimpse of an inspecting General, we have not come very much under the spell of the Army proper. We have copied the way it wears its caps and slings its rifles, and we have puzzled over its knack of getting that neat overlap in its trousers below the knee, but these are superficialities unlikely to lead to any deeper understanding. Recently, however, thanks to the zeal of an ambitious few, more intimate relations have been established between our two forces.

The liaison had its beginnings in the cordial atmosphere of a public-house a few miles distant, much frequented by real soldiers. It was there that a keen member of "D" Section became friendly, towards the end of the evening, with no less a personage than a Sergeant-major. It transpired that this Sergeant-major would condescend, if asked nicely, to give our platoon a hint or two about winning the war, and the news was hurried home to our Section Leaders, who lost no time in putting negotiations in train.

When we of the rank and file heard of this windfall we were flattered and a little touched to think that a busy warrior, with many calls on his time and temper, should be willing to squander the one and risk total loss of the other, with nothing as his reward but a promise of free transport both ways; and when it became known that our platoon was only one of several benefiting from his lofty altruism, our admiration for the man soared giddily. This was the spirit, we said to ourselves, that was going to whack the Axis.

However, when our Section Leader asked him, on his first visit, how on earth he found time to do so much for so many, he replied with a slight air of surprise that he had nothing else to do; was, in fact, attached to the Home Guard officially. This revelation exploded our theories about his lovable nature, but compensated us to a certain extent by swelling our self-esteem. To have a real Sergeant-major attached to us seemed to place us on a higher level altogether, even if the attachment had proved to be official rather than emotional.

It must be admitted that when he eventually stood before us we felt a vague chill of disappointment to find that this was not the Sergeant-major famed in song and story. Here was no fifteen-stone despot with purple complexion, spiky moustache and violent tongue, but a small pale man with smouldering dark eyes and considerable etymological restraint.

We soon learned that his stock-in-trade, in addition to an undoubted grasp of his subject, included a small fund of mild witticisms delivered with no apparent expectancy of applause, and a disconcerting habit of hurling himself like lightning to the ground in order to demonstrate any point that might not be quite clear. His diction displayed that inability to cope successfully with the letter "t" which has done so much to enhance the popularity of Mr. Jack Warner. "Pu' a jerk in i'!" he pleaded, towards the end of his first Sunday morning with us in the Village Hall. "My dinner's all poured ou'!"

This is one of his favourite jests; another, and one which we shall not easily tire of hearing, is to beseech us not to look so worried, as we "ain't doin' i' for a livin'." And this is perhaps the secret of his tolerance towards us. As raw recruits who had accepted the King's shilling instead of Sir Edward Grigg's one-and-sixpence, we should probably have been bullied to death in the first five minutes, but the authorities have obviously told him that we are a touchy lot, entitled to quit in a huff if we feel like it, and have warned him not to provoke us into indulging this valued privilege.

It speaks well for us—or perhaps for some subtle magnetism in him—that we do not take advantage of his gentleness to treat him with anything but deep respect. Even if he does fall a little short of our conception of sergeant-majors as a body, the tradition hallowing his rank forbids that easy familiarity which we adopt towards our own superior officers. Some of the more impressionable of us even address him humbly as "Sir," and a member of "A" Section almost brought a blush to his sallow cheek by calling him "Major" throughout his first address. One young lad who has only recently joined us went a little too far in the other direction and prefaced a question with "I say, Sarge!" The rest of us held our breath, but the lad's only rebuke was a silent and unwavering stare directed at him for the best part of a minute and having excellent effect.

The same telling technique was employed to put our own Mr. Corker in his place, not for any breach of etiquette but because of his tendency to speak freely and exhaustively on any subject that happens to crop up. A burst of vigorous reminiscence about his own army days (when things were done quicker, better and more often) held up the Sergeant-major's discourse for some minutes; when the flow of words had at last died away under that shrivelling gaze, with the inevitable *coda* of ". . . I mean, if you see what I mean, I mean . . ." the Sergeant-major transferred his attention to the remainder of his audience and said, "I'll just repea' tha' bi' abou' the bayone' . . ." The treatment was so effective that there has been talk amongst our Section of trying it on Mr. Corker ourselves sometime, but it is doubtful whether anything will come of it. None of us has quite the right sort of eyes.

When the Sergeant-major talks to us there is a strange atmosphere of the school-room hovering over us all. Once more wondering Ignorance is dazzled by wonderful Knowledge; once more we feel a self-important glow when some special duty exalts us above the rest of the class (lending teacher our rifle, for instance, or hastening to pick up his fallen notebook); and although things have not quite reached the stage when we bring bunches of wild flowers and lay them adoringly before his army boots, there is a scuffle to hand him a cigarette when we are dismissed, and a rivalry for the distinction of driving him home, which must surely be a corresponding adult manifestation of the forgotten homage of youth.

He is a bloodthirsty little man, this khaki-clad schoolmaster, and the invective which he refrains from hurling at our heads is reserved for references to the enemy, singly or in the mass. The invader whose schemes it will be our joy to foil is always described by the Sergeant-major as "—— Jerry," and this without any word of apology or false diffidence. It is "—— Jerry" who is hiding behind the "bushy-topped trees" in the middle distance; "—— Jerry" who is watching for our slightest movement as we lie in the "tussocky grass" in the left foreground; "—— Jerry" who dives from the air on to our scanty cover beside the "rail-and-post fence," or has established a machine-gun nest in the "red-roofed building, right centre." The highly-coloured picture of the English countryside which the Sergeant-major has pinned up on the wall of our classroom is, in fact (and to use his own words), "stinking with —— Jerries." The two main things to remember, he tells us as his last word for the day, are that "—— Jerry" will shoot us if we don't shoot him, and that "—— Jerry" will run a mile at the sight of a bayonet—provided of course that we grimace fiercely enough and shout loudly enough as we run along behind it.

After the first shock to our illusions we found ourselves on the whole much impressed by our Sergeant-major. Some of us are even a little envious. Mr. Punnitt and Mr. Benn, for example, the glory still in their eyes as they watched our Section Leader drive him proudly away to his long-poured-out dinner, both declared that if they had been younger men they would have enlisted without hesitation, purely for the satisfaction of working up to be Sergeant-majors themselves. But little Mr. King, leaning on his bicycle and gazing after the receding car, shook his head doubtfully.

"Ah," said he, with the air of one who knows his limitations, even though others may not—"but 'tain't everyone as can do it. He's got the gift o' the gab, see—aye, and eddication, too!"

Meiosis

A FRIEND of mine from U.S.A.
Said "How I like the English way
Of understating things . . . meiosis . . .
That is, in reasonable doses!
For instance, what a splendid plan
To speak of Hitler as *That Man!*"
"To call him man, it seems to me,"
I answered, "is hyperbole."

o   o

The Long Way Round

"Lord Willingdon, head of the British trade mission to South Africa, Lady Willingdon, and principal members of the mission have reached Santiago, Chile from Uruguay."—*Daily Paper.*

Women Go to War

Women's lives were transformed as they became a crucial part of every aspect of the war effort, from the armed forces to manufacturing, agriculture, transport and the emergency services.

"I want something that puts all that in a nutshell."

THE CHANGING FACE.
XVII. – TROUSERS

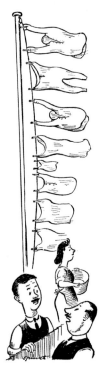

"My wife's on leave – she's in the Wrens."

"Yes, certainly. It's fifteen-thirty-four BST."

*"...and when you go to sea,
I suppose you sit at the
Captain's table."*

*"Sorry – no more, Bert. And if I've gone to
bed you'll find your supper in the oven."*

"A first-class workman's ticket to Hayford, please."

"Next take a tablespoonful of TNT. . . ."

AT THE NEW GEORGE AND DRAGON
"Forty million nice Woolton pies, forty million."

"THEY SHALL PASS"

THE OLD SLOGAN
"Noch einmal – my patience is exhausted!"

THE REAPER

(Food Minister Lord Woolton marks the opening of British Restaurants offering
cheap wholesome meals. Admiral Darlan, Marshal Pétain and Pierre Laval mark
the height of Vichy France's collaboration with the Germans, while Hitler's
invasion of the Soviet Union stalls as winter begins and Stalin exacts revenge.)

"Oh, PERFECTLY safe! We camouflaged MONTHS ago!"

At the Pictures

OVER THERE

UNLESS films about Nazi Germany are poison to you (and that's a point of view), you should find two of the new ones well worth while.

The dramatic ingredients of the first, *Escape* (Director: MERVYN LEROY), are all old; but it is an excellently made and brilliantly exciting melodrama, with many incidents out of the conventional run, and absorbing entertainment. There are particular points of interest too about the playing. Not that ROBERT TAYLOR's part taxes his ability much, or NORMA SHEARER's hers; but the great NAZIMOVA reappears and is impressively good, a new actor from Holland, PHILIP DORN, shows great ability, and ALBERT BASSERMANN, also a refugee from this side of the Atlantic, makes his tiny scene one of the most memorable things in the picture.

The story might be crudely and unfairly described as a sensational trifle about a revivified corpse, but if that puts you in mind of BORIS KARLOFF, forget him. There is nothing cheaply horrific about this piece. It deals with a young American (Mr. TAYLOR) in (pre-war) Germany to find his mother (NAZIMOVA), who made her name as an actress in America but unwisely returned to her native land and broke its peculiar laws. After immense trouble—the conspiracy of fear-stricken silence is very well shown—he hears that she is in a concentration camp about to be executed, and tries frantically to get her out. With the connivance of a doctor (Mr. DORN) who gives her a drug, she is got out as dead, revives and eventually her son escapes with her from the country.

Miss SHEARER's part in all this? She is a *Countess* who runs a sort of finishing-school and helps by hiding them. It is all admirably done and the suspense is terrific. The escape at the end is, I suppose, too easy; but presumably even the Gestapo falls down sometimes.

There is a grimmer and more genuine ring about the ending of *Freedom Radio* (Director: ANTHONY ASQUITH). This film imagines the story behind the "German Freedom Station" that used to broadcast opposition to the Nazis just before and in the early days of

J.H.D.

[*Escape*

Mark Preysing—ROBERT TAYLOR (to *Countess Von Treck*—NORMA SHEARER). "I'm hunting Mamma in the grip of the Gestapo, but' a fella must have a break."

the war; and the ending, though nominally "unhappy"—the organizer and his wife are killed in the act of broadcasting—has a stimulating postscript: their young assistant excitedly takes over on the reserve transmitter. When I was there the audience clapped this; and although their approval was, no doubt, for the spirit of the brave people who do such things, *Freedom Radio* well deserves praise as a piece of film-making too. It is full of excellently contrived moments, and the familiarity of the incidentals—grim foxy Gestapo men, marching troops, the misery of poor people who unluckily do something illegal, the brutalization of ordinary pleasant youths—has no tedious effect, for the fresh imaginative touch in the treatment makes all the difference.

The acting too is good. CLIVE BROOK is the doctor, *Karl*, who sets up the secret station; DIANA WYNYARD is his wife *Irena*, an actress at first so in sympathy with the Nazis that she accepts a State appointment. DEREK FARR is extremely effective as the young radio-mechanic *Hans*, and as his ill-fated betrothed, JOYCE HOWARD gives a pleasant and moving performance. RAYMOND HUNTLEY is overwhelmingly sinister in a sort of Himmler part.

We get back to the British atmosphere in *You Will Remember* (Director: JACK RAYMOND), a touched-up biography of the song-composer LESLIE STUART: gentle fun in the utmost good taste, and a solid background of type-characters. *Stuart* himself, well-played by ROBERT MORLEY, is no type-character, nor perhaps is his friend *Bob* (EMLYN WILLIAMS); but it has apparently been decided, as always, that no audience would tolerate any unexpected trait in a member of the supporting cast. (I should much like to have the chance of eradicating from any new British film any character capable of being described in the terms "*You* know, one of those people who——") It is a simple story—I don't know how near the facts—of poverty, success, riches, debt, oblivion; the chief reason for it after all is the string of good tunes, and *they*'re all right.   R M.

J.H.DOWD

[*Freedom Radio*

SPILLING THE BEANS

Irena . . . . DIANA WYNYARD
Karl . . . . CLIVE BROOK

"Are these war-time revues all remarkably alike, or do we keep on going to the same show by mistake?"

J.H.DOWD

YOUNG SALTS   *[Sailors Three]*

Johnny · · · · · · · · · · · · · · · · · MICHAEL WILDING
Tommy · · · · · · · · · · · · · · · · · TOMMY TRINDER
Llewellyn · · · · · · · · · · · · · · · CLAUDE HULBERT

"Well, madam, in a way it IS a film about the war, but they'd never allow that to interfere with the love-interest."

NOISE 1841

NOISE 1941

Impressions of Parliament

Business Done

Monday, December 8th.—House of Lords and House of Commons: More History is Made.

Tuesday, December 9th. — House of Commons: National Service Bill Gets an Easy Ride.

Wednesday, December 10th.—House of Commons: The House is Shocked; National Service Bill Again.

Thursday, December 11th.—House of Commons: The Prime Minister Does a Tale Unfold.

Monday, December 8th.—Even so old a Parliamentary hand as your scribe is sometimes a little puzzled (and a lot proud) when he looks on Parliament in crisis. To-day, for instance.

Summoned, at a dozen hours' notice, from the ends of the land, Peers and M.P.s gathered quietly and sat in their respective Chambers waiting—for all the world like well-satisfied shareholders at some prosperous company's annual meeting—for the arrival of Ministers. They gossiped quietly; they showed no sign of excitement.

Into the Commons strode Mr. WINSTON CHURCHILL, fresh from a Cabinet meeting. There was a low cheer.

In the most matter-of-fact tones he

THE LIGHT THAT FLAMES

" We have at least four-fifths of the population of the globe upon our side."

told the story that will assuredly find its place among the blackest pages of human treachery and double-dealing.

The story of how the Japanese Government, while keeping President ROOSEVELT and the Government of the United States busy with assumed hopes of, and plans for, peace, suddenly, on December 7th, 1941, flashed out the assassin's dagger.

While Japanese emissaries actually talked with United States Ministers, Japanese warplanes rained down death and destruction on United States naval bases in the ironically-named Pacific.

And so it fell out that Britain's Parliament was summoned to hear from Mr. CHURCHILL a declaration that, an hour or two before, the Cabinet had implemented his own pledge that if the United States found herself at war with Japan, Britain would be at her side "within the hour."

Confident of the assent of the nation—there was no doubting it in the ringing cheers of its elected representatives—Mr. CHURCHILL had repeated the promise over the Transatlantic telephone to Mr. ROOSEVELT, in the small hours of the morning. He had also sent an encouraging message to Thailand and a promise of the completest aid to China.

A sombre panorama the world presented, said Mr. CHURCHILL, but Japan seemed to have been infected with HITLER'S madness and the root of the evil and its branch must be extirpated together. That must be done—but there must be no underrating the dangers and risks involved, for Japan may have made her attacks because of her confidence of strength, as much as in a fit of recklessness.

But we too had confidence—the supreme confidence of the upholders of right.

The PRIME MINISTER sat down. Mr. LEES-SMITH, Leader of the Opposition-That-Does-Not-Oppose, and Sir PERCY HARRIS, for the Liberals, underlined the complete unanimity of the nation.

As if to add a special underlining of his own, Mr. LESLIE HORE-BELISHA, not always lavish in his praise of HIS MAJESTY'S present advisers, paid graceful tribute to the wisdom and foresight of Mr. CHURCHILL in making naval dispositions in the Far East (blandly described by the Premier as "convenient") against the emergency that had now arisen. Now it must be total war.

With which grim thought the House rose.

Tuesday, December 9th.—Mr. DAVID KIRKWOOD, stormy and impulsive Clydesider, "doubled" the parts of hero and villain of a touching little drama, with Miss ELLEN WILKINSON as heroine and villainess.

Miss WILKINSON, for the Home

Office, was giving some reply to a question, when Mr. KIRKWOOD, brows knitted, was heard to comment on the reply in a way highly derogatory to its veracity. And he preceded his comment with a big, big D.

The House was horrified and said so. Miss WILKINSON merely smiled her

Sergeant Bevin : " Squad—'Shun ! "

"The British people is 'an awkward squad.' "
The Minister of Labour.

sunniest smile. Mr. Speaker was afflicted with his famous tactful deafness.

Then Mr. KIRKWOOD, ever the most gallant of men, rose up and explained that he wished to cast no aspersions on the truthfulness of "*her Ladyship.*" Could graceful apology go further? The House roared its forgiveness, while Mr. KIRKWOOD was heard to declaim that the statement was "inaccurate all the same." The curtain descended to deafening cheers.

Sir JOHN GRAHAM KERR made inquiries about a Government Advisory Committee on Camouflage, which has apparently done its job so effectively that nobody has seen it for months. Rear-Admiral BEAMISH wanted the church bells (now invasion signals) sounded on Christmas Day as a tribute to the efficiency of the Home Guard, but Mr. ATTLEE, for the PRIME MINISTER, said "No!" very firmly.

Mr. RUPERT DE LA BERE, who has a sort of slogan that "the entire matter is most unsatisfactory," caused astonishment by rising, bowing, and saying "Thank you, very much," to Captain DAVID MARGESSON simply because he

"I'm sorry you don't like it, Sir – it's the only one we've got left."

said there *was* War Office co-operation with the Minister of Labour over the calling up of men.

Then the House went on to consider the Second Reading of the National Service Bill, which puts us all at the disposal of the State. The threatened storm over its passage was lost in the cyclone sweeping from Tokyo, and so calm was it all that the Second Reading was according without so much as a division.

Wednesday, December 10th.—Again that superb sang-froid—this time in face of news that would certainly have shaken most human assemblies.

White, but with his lips set in a firm line, Mr. CHURCHILL hurried into the Commons, with Mr. ALEXANDER, his First Lord of the Admiralty, in close attendance. He had heard over breakfast some news that could not be held, and he obtained the SPEAKER's permission to make a statement as soon as the House sat.

Straight into it he plunged: "I have bad news." The House sat silent. "The battleship *Prince of Wales* and the *Repulse* have been sunk, according to reports from Singapore."

That was all. The House gave its low cheer, this time in the tones of sympathy. Mr. CHURCHILL rose, went from the Chamber.

Grimly determined, the House dealt with the committee stage of the National Service Bill.

Thursday, December 11th. — Mr. CHURCHILL would have made (or

should it be does make?) a great impresario.

He presents himself, on important occasions, with a skill that would make most men green with envy.

To-day he told the story of the successful Battle of Libya, of the strikingly changed position in Russia, of the grim conflict in the Pacific, of the heartening battle of the Atlantic. It was all superbly told, as a running drama, with a sincere tribute to Admiral Sir TOM PHILLIPS, whose flagship was *Prince of Wales*, as climax.

The fact that he added the most interesting details in reply to questions from Sir ROGER KEYES and others did not greatly detract from a polished literary effort.

Sir PERCY HARRIS asked wistfully for a secret session — there having been none for several days—but received little support.

Friday, December 12th.—The House of Lords, having received the National Service Bill from the Commons overnight, sat specially to-day to ensure that no time was lost in passing it into law. There was a brief debate, the Second Reading was passed, and that was that.

"By the way, did you remember to feed the canary?"

"I can remember the days when this bit of London was entirely uninhabited."

SUN AND WIND

" Japan is at present at the cross-roads."—*Admiral Tojo*.

THESE DEAD . . . SHALL NOT HAVE DIED IN VAIN.

"You have a greater task than I had. Slavery must be removed from the whole of the earth."

(After Japan's attack on Pearl Harbor on December 7, America was at
war. Days later Germany and Italy declared war on the USA.)

1942

A World at War

"... and you can tell your General that's MY opinion. This ain't a soldier's war
– it's a PEOPLE's war, this is!

"I shall have to have tomorrow off, Mr Boom – I've to
answer a summons for being away yesterday."

"You're going overseas, mate – that's all I can tell yer."

THE NEWSPAPER BATTLE SCHOOL

"And those behind cried 'Forward!'"
And those in front cried 'Back!'"

"Are you sure this is Lord Woolton pie, Jennie?"

When John Smith gets away on leave –

a subtle change takes place:

the same is true of his sister Joan –

only rather different.

"We went down to a few INCHES."

"And as for your taunt about getting on with the war, I assure you that nobody is more anxious to win the war than I am."

"And what else does your mother want for her birthday, dear, besides a nice piece of haddock?"

"No standing on top please."

Land Girls

The Women's Land Army had originally been established in the First World War. In June 1939, with farmers urged to increase food production as the prospect of shortages loomed, coupled with the loss of manpower to the armed forces, help in agriculture was a priority and the Land Army was revived. By 1943 more than 80,000 women were working in farming. At first regarded with misgivings by their rural employers, the Land Girls soon showed their worth, carrying out gruelling work in all weathers.

"Now would be a good time to whitewash his stall, Gladys."

"I wonder what's become of Mary?"

THE FARMER'S IDEA OF THE LANDGIRL

THE LANDGIRL'S IDEA OF THE FARMER

Impressions of Parliament

Business Done

Tuesday, May 12th.—House of Lords: Pieces of Austerity are Announced.

House of Commons: Some More Pieces. Coal Plan is Scuttled.

Wednesday, May 13th. — House of Commons: The Finance Bill in Committee.

Tuesday, May 12th.—The Lachrymose Order of Austerity and the Anti-Austerity League (or whatever it is) struggled for mastery in both Houses to-day.

Lord WOOLTON, Food Minister, told their Lordships that his instalment of Austerity was to limit restaurant-meal prices. When he went on to explain that the limit might be as high as 16*s.* 6*d.* per meal, per person, per visit, exclusive of drinks, noble Lords appeared puzzled to assess the precise degree of Austerity involved in a price of that order.

The Food Minister seemed pleased with the scheme. Most of the other Members of the Gilded Chamber affected neutrality, so all went merrily as a marriage-bell.

Bells, incidentally, were the subject of an attempted Anti-Austerity blitz by Petty-Officer A. P. HERBERT in the Commons. *He* wanted the church bells to ring out again, irrespective and regardless of the modern meaning and significance of that once-joyous sound. But War Minister Sir JAMES GRIGG (who *looks* austere, but possesses one of the most refreshingly-breezy senses of humour in the entire House) said No.

Church bells, said he, thrusting out his jaw, had been given the war-time rôle of invasion alarms, and invasion alarms they must stay, though all the might of the Merrie-Englanders be arrayed against the idea.

But back to our ermine. In the Lords, Austerity High-Priest WOOLTON was in action again, this time *repelling* an attack of Austerity from that renowned teetotaller, Lord ARNOLD. That nobleman wanted beer rationed. Under the disapproving glances of his peers, he asked that, in these days when solid food is rationed with increasing severity, beer should also be cut—or whatever the process is with liquids.

Lord ARNOLD sat down, hope and fear written in letters of equal size on his countenance. Lord WOOLTON rose up, determination and stern resolution inscribed on his.

Only, he said (in effect), over my dead, bleeding and battered body will you touch beer—at any rate in an unfriendly way! Lay not an infidel hand on the Sacred Hop! Noble Lords looked a little astonished at the vehemence of the defence.

Then (if your scribe may be permitted, so to say, to mix his drinks) they perceived the milk in the coconut. "*I do not propose to add to the problems of the Government* by rationing beer," he said. Evidently beer would be one over the eight for the Government.

As for the social results of beer (using the word generically), there had been a pretty steep decline in convictions for drunkenness since the war began. Lord WOOLTON clearly thought this a tribute to the strength of will of the drinkers; many of his hearers as clearly ascribed it to the weakness of the drink.

Lord ELTON, whose speech—the adage notwithstanding—is as golden as his mellifluous voice is silvern, delighted the House with a moving plea against that other hotly-contested piece of Government Austerity, fuel rationing.

Officially organized darkness and cold was no offering for a gallant long-suffering nation such as ours, he said, and went on to draw a harrowing picture of the lot of the unhappy housewife, hunted and harried by meter-readers, coalmen, and other Questing Beasts intent on her coupons.

He proceeded to give a sort of zoological lecture on the genus *Meter-readerii* ("I do not know how many of your Lordships may have encountered one"), explaining they were to be found frequenting back-doors, little places under the stairs, and the back-ends of garages. Their task was to read a couple of figures and then return to their burrows—or was it forms?

Lord GAINFORD, who was furious about something, added some pungent criticism of fuel rationing, and Lord SNELL, given the thankless task of defending the Government's supposed plans, poured apparently unrationed (fuel) oil on the troubled waters, and advised everyone to wait and see.

Back in the Commons Sir JAMES GRIGG was administering a dose of Austerity, neat, to the Home Guard, saying H.G.s were not permitted to buy at N.A.A.F.I.s and the like, tobacco and cigarettes free of additional duty, as were Regular soldiers.

This did not go so well in a House crowded with khaki-clad Palace of Westminster Home Guards, waiting to be inspected, at a foundation-anniversary parade, by the PRIME MINISTER. But they all put on "We-can-take-it" expressions, and added this newest weight to their rapidly-growing equipment.

Wednesday, May 13th.—An unlucky day for the fuel-rationing plan. Sir STAFFORD CRIPPS, who a week earlier had proclaimed coal rationing as the last word in perfection, had to announce that it was to be scuttled for the time being, and that its operation from June 1 was out of the question.

NATIONAL DRINKS—II

"The larger barrelage now being drunk consists of extra water—a beverage approved by the highest authorities."—*Lord Woolton.*

The Conservatives cheered. But the Labour men looked grim, and it was clear that Mr. GORDON MACDONALD voiced their general view when he said that they wanted a look-in while the scheme was being amended. Sir STAFFORD promised that the new scheme (if and when) would incorporate plans for better production and organization of the coal industry as well as for a cut in consumption.

The shadow of Nationalization being thus skilfully painted into the picture by Parliament's most expert artist, Members were left fearing (or hoping, according to predilections), to await the new scheme, due to be produced some time post-Whitsun.

The Budget claimed the attention of the House again, with Sir KINGSLEY WOOD, Chancellor of the Exchequer, beaming his benedictions on all movers and seconders of amendments, and maledictions on their amendments. All—bene *and* mal—with the most seraphic of smiles.

BIGGER AND MORE BEAUTIFUL BUDGETS

"I find the work delightful."

(Sir Kingsley Wood, Chancellor of the Exchequer, announced his fifth
war budget on April 14: estimated expenditure £5,286,000,000.)

ONE HUNDRED PER CENT.

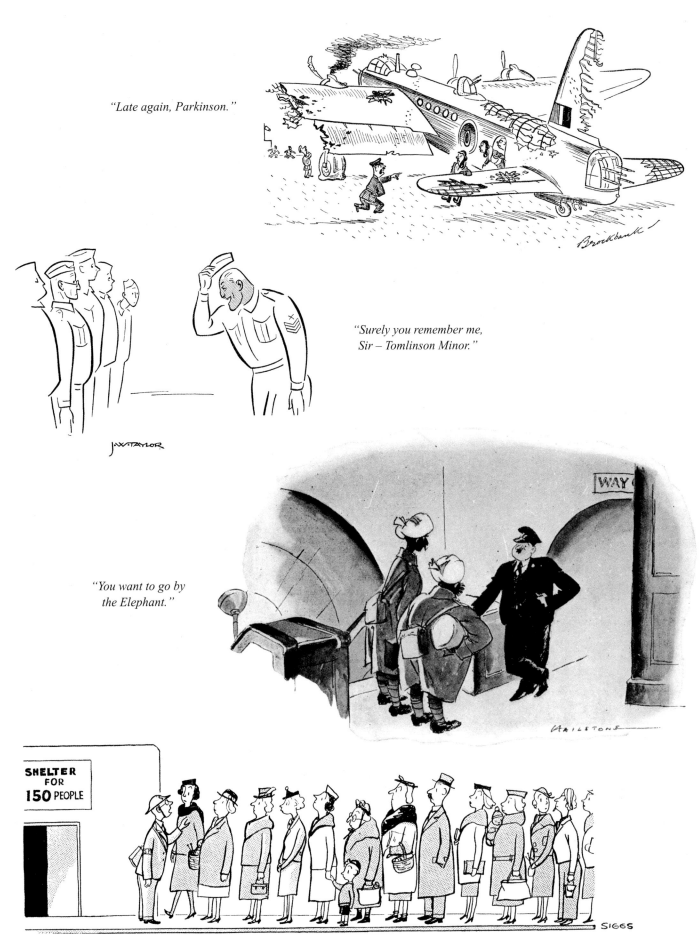

"Late again, Parkinson."

"Surely you remember me,
Sir – Tomlinson Minor."

"You want to go by
the Elephant."

"You can't go in yet; there's only forty-seven of you."

133

SALUTE TO THE BRAVE

"THE SEA-KING'S BROTHERS FROM OVER THE SEA"

THE OFFER
"That's not a white flag. It has a dirty smudge on it."

SPOIL OF THE HILLS

(Britain had many Allies in the struggle against the Axis Powers. France
and Britain stood together to aid Poland against Germany. Others ranged
from Norway and Greece to the partisans of Yugoslavia.)

DRAMATIC MOMENTS
OR THE GRUESOME TRAGEDY OF BENITO MACBETH
"Is that a digger that I see behind me?"

WAITING FOR THEIR HOUR

FREEDOM ON THE HEIGHTS
[In admiration of the mountain guerilla army still fighting
against Germany and Italy on Yugo-Slav soil.]

THE GATE OF INDIA

(The armed forces of the Empire were first to offer support – among
them troops from Australia, Canada and India.)

"'Borough of Grimstone' calling 'Metal-Workers Guild' and 'Ethels of Empire'."

Parrots and the R.A.F.

III

THE R.A.F. Mess, Prangmere, thought it had really got rid of Flying-Officer Flaps' parrot last week, when the bird broke off an ill-advised combat with the Mess cat and disappeared into the night—the cat subsequently claiming a probable. Yesterday, however, the parrot—described by Squadron-Leader Undercart as a grey mid-wing monoplane with heavily armoured front turret, retractable undercarriage and high yellow astrodome—made a silent glide approach through the window and began to circle the aerodrome prior apparently to coming in to land.

The Mess promptly went into committee.

Pilot-Officer Airscrew said blow him down, if it wasn't that damn parrot again. Flying-Officer Flaps said hell's bells, and he had been hoping it had force-landed somewhere out in the wilds and broken its ruddy neck. Pilot-Officer Prune said parrots didn't break their necks when they force-landed. Flying-Officer Flaps said they would if they forgot to select their undercarriage down, they'd belly-land, tilt up on their nose and . . . Pilot-Officer Prune said parrots never broke their necks at any time, they hadn't that sort of air-frame, they could only get them wrung. Flying-Officer Flaps took a poor view of Pilot-Officer Prune's theory, referring to it as complete bull.

The parrot said cronklechawkleookerchonk, or words to

that effect, and began to hover above the recumbent form of Flight-Lieutenant Lyne-Shute having a zizz on the settee after a late night in the Ops Room. Pilot-Officer Airscrew said what did it say, and Flying-Officer Talespin said its R/T didn't seem to be very good but he thought it was asking what was its turn to land, please. Squadron-Leader Undercart said good lord, it's mistaken Flight-Lieutenant Lyne-Shute's stomach for the flare-path, here, wake up, Lyne-Shute! . . . Wing-Commander Blower hastily said not to tell him, for heaven's sake, it'd spoil it, give the bird a green on the Aldis lamp and see what happened. Pilot-Officer Rudder said cracking fine idea, Sir, and Pilot-Officer Nosedyve said a-absolutely wizard.

The parrot made an engine-assisted approach, held off nicely at three inches, and made a perfect three-pointer landing without over-shooting the boundary of Flight-Lieutenant Lyne-Shute's tunic.

Flight-Lieutenant Lyne-Shute said abruptly eeayeoh*ow*. The parrot said what a night, what a night, took off hastily and went round again. Flight-Lieutenant Lyne-Shute asked what the suffering sam was that. Flying-Officer Talespin said what was his trouble. Flight-Lieutenant Lyne-Shute thanked him and said his was a beer, and as he (Talespin) was nearest the bell . . .

The parrot set a course for the far end of the Mess, did a snappy Immelman just above the radio and made good a reciprocal track to the fire-place end, where Group-Captain Boost was reading the paper.

Pilot-Officer Rudder said oh, Sir, look out, Sir, and covered his eyes. The parrot just banked round Group-Captain Boost's head in time, using a lot of rudder, and calling up Aerodrome Control, requested them to roll out the barrel.

Group-Captain Boost said what was that, was it that infernal parrot again, shoot it down someone and put it back in its hangar, it looked as though it were going to dive-bomb him any minute. Squadron-Leader Undercart said he thought it was only making dummy runs. Flight-Lieutenant Lyne-Shute, hastily finishing his beer, said he for one was taking no chances, down the hatch, Talespin, old man, but let's have the other half.

The parrot pointed out that in its opinion there'd be no promotion this side of the ocean, so cheer up, its lads . . . Squadron-Leader Undercart here winged it with a match-box and its R/T luckily packed up. Pilot-Officers Airscrew

"Yes, I pulled the cord. The wheels kept saying: 'Is your journey really necessary? Is your journey really necessary? Is your journey really necessary...?' I just couldn't stand it any longer."

"Despise Not Prophesying . . ."

IF, in 1933,
you had said to me
Virginia, old sock, I see it all planned,
it is written in your horoscope and in your hand
that in 1942
you
will find yourself sitting one night,
feeling quite
outstandingly pipped
in the crypt
of a Bristol church . . . you will be leaning in a dump
over an object called a stirrup pump,
wearing your husband's trousers and a travelling rug,
and drinking tepid coffee out of an enamel mug——
  Stop! I should have said,
listen, my sweet, you are ill, you must go to bed
at once! Now don't get in a rage,
but it looks as if you're getting to the pink elephant stage,
so be a good chap and throttle
down on the bottle.
  Or I might have said Chucks!
or Sucks!
but I should never, never,
however
much it grieved you,
have said I believed you.

Which only goes to show,
said she, again (alas) rolling off the lie-low.   V. G.

o   o

Now You Know

"Once again this week-end the world's spotlight turns to Tokyo, where Japanese statesmen are again grappling with problems engendered by attempting to follow a national policy whose repercussions tend to exceed the limits set by circumspection."—*Malta Paper.*

and Rudder next came into action with heavy flak—magazines and books from the Mess table—and for some while the barrage was intense. The parrot took skilful avoiding action throughout and Pilot-Officer Nosedyve said it would be wizard on an operational sortie. Wing-Commander Blower said that he'd like to see it over Hamburg. Group-Captain Boost said personally he intended to see it in its cage or know the reason why, get cracking now. Flight-Lieutenant Lyne-Shute said whoever threw that Bradshaw would have to buy him another beer.

At this point the parrot came down low and began hedge-hopping the chairs. A lucky burst from a rolled-up *Express* (Flying-Officer Talespin) caused it to crash-land in an armchair. Squadron-Leader Undercart, operating the heaviest flak yet seen—a cushion—said got it, dammit he hadn't, yes by Jove he had, it was underneath, pull it out someone. Four Pilot-Officers and one Flying-Officer pointed out it was Flying-Officer Flaps' parrot. Flying-Officer Flaps said the hell with that, its front gunner was still in action and he'd been bitten three times already, let it have a taste of someone else.

Group-Captain Boost said he'd give Flying-Officer Flaps just five minutes, what about it?

Flying-Officer Flaps thereupon returned the bird to its hangar with a skilful grip on the top of the fuselage. The parrot said a large number of things which would have been quite unrepeatable except that Flying-Officer Flaps on releasing it became a casualty for the fourth time and repeated most of them.

Flight-Lieutenant Lyne-Shute said he'd like very much to know who *did* throw that Bradshaw, and the committee meeting was then terminated.   A. A.

Yanks

The first American troops arrived in Britain on January 26, 1942 and the Yanks were to be a source of fascination and cultural misunderstandings over the years that followed.

"Gee, this is nothing – you ought to have seen the way we imagined it over in the States."

"Don't forget, Beryl – the response is 'Hiya, fellers!' and a sort of nonchalant wave of the hand."

"They won't let on who the camp is for."

"No, I can't remember that we ever did celebrate Magna Carta day."

"Anyone else in the class a gum-chum of our
American allies?"

1939

1941

"Calm yourself, dear. Even Hitler can't be both dregs AND scum."

"How many salutes for a general, Charlie?"

141

Impressions of Parliament

Business Done

Tuesday, June 23rd.—House of Lords:
The Convoy Gets Through.
   House of Commons: Premonitory
Symptoms.
Wednesday, June 24th.— House of
Commons: Oliver's Travels—a Short
Story.
Thursday, June 25th.—House of Com-
mons: Secret Upon Secret.

Tuesday, June 23rd.—The Censor
can have no objection to your scribe's
recording that to-day Ministers turned
up their coat-collars (metaphorically)
and blew (figuratively) on their fingers,
so cold was the atmosphere in the
House of Commons.

This was no reflection on the
excellent work of Messrs. HOLMAN
and HATTERSLEY, Parliament's own
Clerks of Works, whose task it is,
behind the scenes, to ensure that
Members are warm (or cool) and able
to see. It was spiritual cold that
afflicted the Treasury Bench—nasty,
icy, bone-chilling blasts that are so
much more difficult to endure than the
most scorching of controversial fires.

Old Parliamentary hands know
that icy atmosphere. It is the most
dangerous and ominous of all Parliamentary temperatures. It comes
before a storm.

Mr. CLEMENT ATTLEE, Deputy
Prime Minister, had to take charge,

"IMPERIUM ET LIBERTAS"

Mr. Harold Macmillan makes his maiden
speech as Parliamentary Under-Secretary
for the Colonies.

Mr. WINSTON CHURCHILL being otherwise engaged in Washington. And
Mr. CLEMENT ATTLEE patently did
not enjoy the situation. He fingered
his papers, read them through and
through, and glanced with alternate
hope and hopelessness at the long
closely-packed ranks opposite.

For he had an unpleasant story to

tell. It was the story of the sudden
swoop of German General ROMMEL
(overnight dubbed Field Marshal by a
grateful HITLER) on much-beleaguered
Tobruk, in Libya, and of the fall
of that town, with 25,000 or more
British troops and untold quantities of
equipment. The fight had seemed to
be going our way, and Mr. CHURCHILL,
a week or two earlier, had expressed
the view that we had a right to be
"more than satisfied" with it.

Then, abruptly as is the way with
modern war, the whole thing went
wrong. ROMMEL had almost knocked
himself out by the vigour of his own
lunge—but we were not able to take
advantage of the fact and push him
right over. In fact we did not push
him at all, he pushed us—and Mr.
ATTLEE had the unhappy task of
trying to explain how it had all
happened.

Like Mr. CHURCHILL earlier, Mr.
ATTLEE preferred to read a report
from General AUCHINLECK, Army
commander in Libya. This told the
now all-too-familiar story of bad luck
and overwhelming.

The House listened in stony silence.
Mr. ATTLEE sat down, looking for
the first signs of the bursting storm.
There was none. One or two Members got up and asked supplementary
questions, quite quietly and calmly.
Mr. ATTLEE stood up and answered,
looking surprised at the zephyr-
like gentleness of the breeze. He
mentioned that the "battle was not
yet over." No one turned a hair—
although the cliché would normally
have produced a hoot from the
critics. Then (hopefully) he trotted
out the clichiest of all clichés about
"moral superiority over the enemy."
Stonier and icier silence.

Baffled, Mr. ATTLEE sat down once
more, having offered a full debate as
soon as this could fruitfully be held.
Lord WINTERTON, without raising
his voice, announced that Mr. CHURCH-
ILL, as Minister of Defence, was
responsible for the state of affairs
revealed, and said he should want a
full statement on how it occurred.
Thus encouraged, Mr. ARTHUR GREEN-
WOOD, leading the Opposition, said
he should demand a debate without
undue delay, and Sir PERCY HARRIS,
the Liberal leader, asked for strict
rationing of "official soothing-syrup"
on this and all other topics.

So far, so puzzling. There was
everybody looking grim, nobody saying anything much to match the facial
expressions.
Sir JOHN WARDLAW-MILNE rose
slowly, adjusted his monocle with
elaborate calm, and confided that he

and his friends would desire to table
a motion of no-confidence in the
central direction of the war. Never
was a vote of censure on a Govern-

SIR WARDLAW DE MILNE
throweth down the gauntlet to the
Government.

ment more casually, more gently, put
forward.

A few Members cheered quietly,
with the expressions of occupants of a
dentist's waiting-room. Mr. ATTLEE
looked a bit like the dentist, feeling
grimly for his forceps and drills.
Then, quite suddenly, he went off
the deep end, as dentists will. Red-
dening, he declared that Sir JOHN
was looking for a scapegoat. This
description of the critics' aim drew
a short sharp yell of contradiction,
which Mr. ATTLEE accepted without
protest. Quiet, once more.

Sir JOHN nonchalantly mentioned
that he would pass over "the insinua-
tion" by Mr. ATTLEE, and Mr. JOHN
DUGDALE, from the Socialist benches,
asked that a Russian General be sent
to Cairo to teach us a thing or two.

Lord WINTERTON gleefully moved,
as an amendment, that the General
be sent to the House to become Prime
Minister.

Then—queerest twist in this queer
situation—Sir GEORGE HUME began a
long harangue, appealing for calm, no
panic, and support for everybody.
He got so hot and scarlet about it
that the House, for the first time,
began to show signs of heat and

"Come and help me to fill in this application form for Six Easy Lessons on Filling in Government Forms."

irritation. Sir GEORGE finished his address (which was technically a question) at the top of his voice, with a Greek chorus of protest supplied by Members of all Parties.

And so they left the matter, for the time being, to launch a long discussion on family allowances. Everybody seemed in favour, but Sir KINGSLEY WOOD, the Chancellor of the Exchequer, remarking that the thing would cost money, asked for time to think it over.

Their Lordships saw Admiral-of-the-Fleet Lord CORK and Admiral-of-the-Merchant-Fleet Lord MARCHWOOD fight another of their brilliant actions in defence of merchant seamen. They wanted tuberculosis contracted because of war service in the merchant navy to qualify its victims for a pension.

Lord SIMON, in unwontedly testy mood, said that was precisely what the Bill they were discussing was for.

Noble Lords made incredulous noises, and the LORD CHANCELLOR'S handsome wig fairly bristled with indignation. He acidly disclaimed any intention to be "irrelevant, fraudulent or scandalous," and spoke meaningly of "logic-chopping."

Law-Lord MAUGHAM contradicted everything the LORD CHANCELLOR had said, other Lords joined in the scrap, Lord MARCHWOOD remarked that the fight between the lawyers encouraged him (on the authority of the old saw) to hope that honest folk like merchant seamen would come by their own, and then Lord SIMON agreed to look into the matter again and try to meet the critics.

Wednesday, June 24th.—Apart from a somewhat vigorous questioning of Sir ARCHIBALD SINCLAIR, the Air Minister, about those "air superiority in Libya" claims, the House was listless to-day.

Mr. OLIVER LYTTELTON, Minister of Production, was about to produce a report on *his* visit to the U.S.A. when Mr. JAMES MAXTON intervened with a protest about the length of Ministerial statements which eat into debating time. Members used up five minutes on their protests, and Mr. LYTTELTON, permitted to proceed, drily remarked that his statement would not take so long as the protests. He was not quite correct—it took six minutes.

Mr. MAXTON, also a master of dry humour, inquired naïvely whether, in the vast expanses of the United States, the Minister had encountered the Parliamentary Secretary to the Ministry of War Transport, who had been "roving about there for more than a year." Mr. LYTTELTON replied, as blandly, that he *had* met Sir ARTHUR SALTER.

Then the House went on to discuss Colonial policy, Mr. HAROLD MAC-MILLAN, the Colonial Under-Secretary, opening the debate. Excitement over this topic was exceedingly moderate.

Thursday, June 25th.—The House of Commons went into secret session on a secret report on a secret statement supposed to have been divulged by an M.P. (whose name was kept secret) as a result of a previous secret session.

Then there was a debate on the threatened ruin of the strawberry crop as a result of the fixing of prices.

THE NEW GATES

THE OLD GATES

"But seriously, darling, Mr Morrison has quite definitely killed the gas-mask fashion."

"And here is another gentleman who will tell us why he carries his respirator when we've been told in the interests of rubber economy not to do so."

"Take my seat, Miss – MADAM – SERGEANT."

"Gambling, eh?"

"Well, well, well! If it isn't Mary Jenkins home on leave from the farm."

"I've been kept in."

*"Can I have four days' compassionate leave, Sir?
My mail's caught up with me."*

"Look, Mummy! This is one they teach us!"

THE BULLDOG HAS WINGS.

(Churchill takes to the skies, travelling to the Second Moscow
Conference via Teheran, stopping en route in Egypt to discuss command
change in the Middle East campaign.)

THE BATTLE FOR THE NILE

THE DELIVERER
*"Have no fear: I have come to set you free
from your chains."*

NO FANFARES NOW
*"We should never have let Adolf blow this, there's
a piece of carpet stuck inside."*

SQUANDERING FUEL

(Halting the Axis offensive at Alam El Halfa was a crucial victory in Egypt.
The Japanese offer India deliverance from her colonial oppressors, while the
Battle of Stalingrad drains German resources even as Hitler trumpets victory,
to the dismay of Heinrich Himmler and Joseph Goebbels.)

"The train down was absolutely packed with troops, dear."

C.A.N.T.
(Off Greece)

WE looked at the cloud
And someone on the bridge
Said "Was that thunder?"
Another peal as loud—
And from its lower edge
(So soft and white that it had made him wonder,
Who spoke, the day being cool and clear,
And Zante, on the beam,
Cloud-dappled and as lovely as a dream)
There came a seaplane, sweeping like a bird
So low and near
That we could see the *fasces* on her wings.
Indeed, it was not thunder we had heard
(It was not thunder weather)
But three fleet fighters going hell-for-leather.
With roar of guns out of the cloud they came
And we—who'd often longed to see such things—
Cheered wildly when a little tongue of flame
Licked round her cock-pit; grew; enveloped all;
So that her fall
Was hymned by the wild cheers.
It was no time for tears;
Yet, when the splash
Quenched the bright flame, and left poor wreckage
of the crash
Then suddenly the shouts died on our lips
And silence came among the grim grey ships;
While Zante, on the beam,
Cloud-dappled lay, as lovely as a dream.

Molesworth and the Domestic Problem

Contains: Diary of grandmothers, chars, pies, cups of fresh, cooks and various weeds.

April 17.—Skool break up late chiz owing to spring sowing in mr trimp's allotment and all boys help. No rags or scrambles chiz as mr trimp (headmaster) give tuough pijaw on austerity. He sa all boys to help parents in diffcult times viz do little things in home chiz chiz he must be potty. All boys are browned off at this except fotherington-tomas who highly delited he sa he hope to do BIG things and will bring his mummy posies of daffs and sho willing spirit he is a grate girly and likes dollies. molesworth 2 sa it won't be so bad as he bags cook breakfast which is tuough on the bacon he will eat it all. Overhear deaf master who sa whoopee end of term and buzz latin book secretly at matron. Can he be human?

April 18.—Same old story we go to grans for hols chiz as she jolly tuough and sa maners makyth manne e.g. molesworth 2 not to twizzle knife on table at dinner. Don't blame her acktually becos molesworth 2 sa Who is biggest fool in world? and knife point to her. We wish butler was here he would haf enjoyed it as ushual but he now in R.A.F. (weehee bonk) also housemaid and all maids. Gran sa she only hope mabel drop as many bombs on germany as she did plates in kitchen and we will win war. ernest (dog) think this funny and bark furously he is a weed and gets no better.

April 18–28.—Think about doing little things in home.

April 29.—Determin to HELP in home.

April 29.—Was i wise in this decission?

May 5.—Make up mind. Rise early to make bed but dercid to do later also clean teeth and brush hair. Find mrs winkle (new cook) in kitchen with wizard frizzly smell. i hope to cash in on smell but chiz as it only what the hens haf. mrs winkle highly delited i clean shoes and make wizard joke e.g. too many cooks muck the soup at which she larff hartily. Also she haf daughter (gladys) who do all work and is super sneke she sa oo mum that little boy clening blak boots with the brown chery blossom. Chiz but mrs winkle only larff and pour huge cup of tea also smoke cig. She sa gladys win embroidery prize at orchard road skool and i repli i can well belive it and exit, master of the situation, to buzz morning bricks at tin roof.

May 6.—Gran is peeved i.e. becos she doing nothing to

"I trust you benefited from last week's exercise in unarmed combat."

help old country in hour of peril. She sa if invasion come she do not intend to sta put. All her life she haf never stayed put and she will not start now. She sa when hour strikes she will be out there scorching the earth and all her friends are impressed and drop tuough stitches. molesworth 2 swank he will be a quisling and boo to everbode he is browned off becos only one slice of the ginger for tea.

May 7.—Gran sa she haf such nice letter from mrs fotherington-tomas and david being a perfect little angel in house. Too early to make statement on this communique.

May 8.—Dercid to help agane with shoes etc. Find mrs winkle who lie on sofa with cig reading racing and football news while gladys do all work e.g. she scrub floor and sa oo mum is it not good to be working she is like wee nell in chatterbox. Start tuough clening of all shoes but chiz as molesworth 2 come in he is afraid i am at bacon or other food. molesworth 2 sa let me help o you might and when i tell him to buzz off he sa fool and i sa million fools. mrs winkle highly delited she sa kick him in the stumick like the wrestlers do but gladys sa i don't fite or sa harsh words do i mum she is a weed. Dercid to tuough up molesworth 2 but he smell chicken food and zoom away to cheat hens. gladys sa each temptation resisted is feather in an angel's wing and mrs winkle is amazed.

May 10.—Find text on pillow. He who refranes is thrice blest. Who can haf done this?

May 11.—Gran take us to weedy concert at happy home canteen chiz chiz chiz as she sa i am to do famous imitation of hitler. i sa no dash it all but gran repli imitation is super and admired by all who haf seen it gosh am i that good? All soldiers browned off at thort of concert they eat sossages dejectedly. Start off fercely shake fists moostash tremble all hairs stand on end but chiz as i friten baby in second row also come to JOKE but noone larff until moostash

drop off chiz then pandermonium and all cheer. molesworth 2 blub he haf not been asked to pla faire bells on piano and all soldiers agane sunk in misery. molesworth 2 begin to pla mightily sossages fly into air mashed potatoes leap like pancakes ham sanwiches fly apart and soldiers deeply impressed it is like the noise of battle. Gran leave note that she unable to make final speech. Also she doubt whether anyone else will be able if molesworth 2 pla faire bells anything like he ushually do.

May 12.—Find next text on toothmug whiteness is the coat of love. Whose is this poison pen?

May 14.—Back to kitchen for work and find mrs winkle with cup of tea and gladys who blak grate delitedly. Also molesworth 2 who very grim as he making woolton pie. gladys sa oo mum just look at what the little boy is doing but mrs winkle sa don't fret she glad to see him enjoying his tiny self cheers cheers cheers she haf hit the nail on the head. molesworth 2 cook mightily pie buble and tremble pastry sizzle flames lick hungrily and all are delited gosh wizard. mrs winkle sa a teaspoon of treacle would burn up nice she is in fits she can hardly drink her tea on account of it being a whole week's wasted.

May 15.—Overhere gran who tell frend that mrs winkle a good little worker. Coo.

May 16.—Sun shine hurra for criket and blossoms of nature. Everbode is feeble and weedy for evermore. Aim crokey ball at ernest (dog) make gran applepie sa boo to mrs winkle and pute molesworth 2 in hen food becos he swank he is a chicken. Only gladys remane. Give her wizard text viz girls are feeble and she so shocked she will not speke to me and peace descends.

May 17.—Tra-la for sumer and birds nesting.

the end.

". . . and the basic ration will all be over by June, and your car will stand idle and deteriorate, and the battery will corrode, and your tyres will get mouldy, and everything will rust and fall to bits."

TRANSFORMATION SCENE

"Avaunt, foul sprite! and be no longer seen
I'll have you know I am the Fairy Queen!"

(William Beveridge's report on reforming Britain's social policies, which
was to form the basis of the post-war welfare state, receives overwhelming
support from the public.)

"How much is the 'No coupons required'?"

"If only they'd tell us all what to do."

"Shall we join the ladies?"

1943

THE TURNING TIDE

"I should think there are more effective ways of saving cloth than by abolishing turn-ups."

"I was doing post-war planning, my boy, before you were born!"

THE DESERT FERRET

(General Bernard Montgomery sends in the crack Eighth Army to flush
out the enemy in the Tunisian Campaign.)

"I'm goin' back – I've forgot me teeth!" "Blimey! They're droppin' bombs, not sandwiches!"

"Them's your Sealed Orders – not to be opened till you're past Camden Town."

"Actually I've a letter of authority here from the Ministry of Home Security permitting me to have turn-ups on my trousers."

"Tell me, tell me, where are you sailing – shipmates o' mine?"

"Doris sends her love and has asked me to play 'Deep in the Heart of Texas' as a reminder of them all at Shepherd's Bush."

"I AM the manager."

"I'm afraid the Regional Commissioner has roped us in for ANOTHER blasted exercise, so I want you all to be on your toes and show him how keen we are."

"... *frightfully behind schedule* HE *is.*"

PUNCH

OR
THE LONDON CHARIVARI

Vol. CCIV   No. 5317   January 13 1943

Charivaria

"My husband, always an enthusiastic cyclist, gave it up after running over a dog in the black-out," states a housewife. It put him off.

o   o

"Fuehrer Fatter," says a heading. His doubles now receive priority food-coupons to catch up.

"I have never tasted anything like British beer," says a U.S. Army officer. He has arrived too late.

o   o

Alexander Dourof, a Russian sword-swallower, states that sword-swallowing does not entail fasting or other preparations. Still, safety-razor blades would be a cheaper diet.

o   o

A table-tennis player won a championship contest on her birthday. Many happy returns.

o   o

We hear that an American soldier visited a London hair-dressing saloon and had a trim, singe, shampoo, massage and shave and bought a packet of razor-blades. Leading up to the blades in this way might be worth trying.

o   o

Inference

"The statement that the convoy was small is presumed to mean that the size of the party which forced its way ashore was not large."—*Australian Paper*.

o   o

A South American woman who swallowed a handful of iron-filings in a quart of water was taken to hospital, where she is expected to recover. There the matter rusts for the moment.

Army recruits are now being given bayonet-fighting instruction on the lines of shadow-boxing. Trained to stick at nothing.

o   o

"When a young author has finished a novel he should have it read aloud to him," says a critic. This may effect a cure.

o   o

Husband Makes Good.

"Then came the great day when an ingenious young Tasmanian built a radio from scraps of wife, solder and old tins."
Daily Paper.

o   o

A man has played the tin whistle for ten years at one London street corner. His takings have increased lately through an arrangement made with a nearby restaurant to act as a cover charge.

o   o

"Citizens of the Reich are confused by the communiqués from the Eastern Front," says a writer. Nevertheless, one predominant fact emerges—the German advance on Rostov continues.

o   o

A comic clockwork figure of MUSSOLINI is on sale in America. Very realistic—even to the wind up.

o   o

"Hitler's Ears Are Burning," says a headline. The beginning of the end?

o   o

Protesting against complaints of over-charging, London taxi-drivers declare that only a few outsiders are guilty. Fare's fair.

o   o

In Germany fishmongers are often offered cast-off clothing in exchange for fish. This is what is called setting a spat to catch a mackerel.

Impressions of Parliament

Business Done

Tuesday, February 16th. — House of Commons: Beveridge Report.

Wednesday, February 17th. — House of Commons: More Explosions.

Thursday, February 18th. — House of Commons: A Muffled Noise.

Tuesday, February 16th.—Alice never never quite lost her wonderment about Wonderland. Your scribe, after twenty years amid the highly-specialized atmosphere of Parliament, has not lost any of his wonderment over the ways and whims of that venerable institution.

Take to-day's proceedings. There we were, all ready for a nice friendly chat over the Beveridge Report, with Mr. ARTHUR GREENWOOD moving a motion that not even the most finicky and pernickety of Government Chief Whips could object to, and everything going as merrily as an invasion bell—when, suddenly, hey presto! the whole place went up in smoke and hard crool words.

It was not as if anybody had sprung a surprise on anybody. Sir JAMES GRIGG, the War Minister, who has an almost Oriental gift for pithy truths, clearly warned the House (admittedly in another connection) that "if we had

LEFT-WING THREE-QUARTERS?

MR. QUINTIN HOGG (Cons.)

to remove all the anomalies in this world it would take a very long time." And yet . . . But perhaps it would be better to begin at the beginning.

Well, there we were, all ready for the aforementioned friendly chat. Mr. GREENWOOD, who is full of knowledge

of the wiles of Government Whips, had tabled a motion that was so indefinite that it was acceptable to the Government. It merely said (in a number of words) that the Beveridge Report was a good idea, worth looking at some time.

To this, seven amendments, all in much more precise terms (and correspondingly unacceptable to the Government) had been put down. One wanted the Report, the whole Report, and nothing but the Report—and quickly. Another wanted the Report put off until the Hitlerian Kalends, or later. Others wanted or did *not* want the Report.

The moment questions were over Lord WINTERTON was up with a request to Mr. Speaker to indicate which of the amendments he intended to call for debate. "Several of them," said he, with that gift for understatement that makes him so considerable a Parliamentarian, "are rather more definitive and objective than the original motion."

"Yes," said Mr. Speaker, "but I do not intend to call *any* of them."

So on went the debate. Mr. MAISKY, the Soviet Ambassador, leaned over to miss no word. Mr. SHINWELL, on the Opposition Front Bench, leaned even further over to miss no word either—although for a different reason, as will appear.

Mr. GREENWOOD was as definite as anybody but a Minister could wish in his demand for decisive and speedy action on the Report. Some unkind person or persons intervened with the query: "Why not say so in your motion?" but Mr. GREENWOOD noticed not the interruption.

Ignoring the Government order that hire-purchase is to cease for the duration, he asked that the Beveridge Plan should be given to a grateful nation "in instalments."

"Why instalments?" bawled the Back-Bench barrackers bellicosely.

"Because," explained their patient leader, momentarily forgetting the ancient rule about addressing the Chair and swinging round on them, "if we do not get it in instalments, we shall not get it at all!"

The objectors looked as if they had heard of people who did not keep up their instalments, but did not pursue the subject. Mr. GREENWOOD, as if reminded of such sordid things by this interlude, mentioned that "pounds, shillings and pence have become meaningless symbols."

Sir KINGSLEY WOOD, the Chancellor of the Exchequer, murmured something that sounded like "Oh, yeah?" and Conservative Members muttered things that sounded much more

definite. Mr. GREENWOOD described finance as the "handmaiden" of industry, and then as its "master," whereupon an irreverent supporter supposed audibly that finance must be a blinkin' harumfrodite.

Then the debate drifted into—well,

ANDERSONIUS SUPERBUS, DECAPITATOR

a debate—until the time came for Sir JOHN ANDERSON, Lord President of the Council, to give the Government's views. Sir JOHN is a thorough person, and he had taken what appeared to be a verbatim note of Mr. GREENWOOD's speech. When he went to the table, he added about fifty foolscap sheets to his already considerable pile, coughed and began.

The Government intended to accept most of the provisions of the Beveridge Report, he said, and intended to make the plan work—"We really *do!*" This statement produced the usual crop of questions and, these over, Sir JOHN said the Report would be implemented when we could see our financial road more clearly—in other words, when the war was over and we had laid the foundations of restored trade and sure employment.

Which might be considered to be reasonable enough and equivalent to the well-tried (if not perhaps very modern or progressive) method of putting in one's foundations before erecting a house on them.

But not at all. The catechism became a caterwauling, and Sir JOHN (most courteous of men) had to appeal for "ordinary courtesy" from Mr. ANEURIN BEVAN, who seemed to be on the verge of hysteria, and several times emitted

"Dear Mother, I can't tell you where I am, but I am somewhere in England."

shrieks of laughter in the most unlikely places. Others joined in the shouts and counter-shouts, with Sir JOHN interjecting an occasional reproof or appeal, an even more occasional item of his speech.

It came to this: As much as we can as soon as we can—when and if we can afford it.

Mr. SHINWELL, Mr. BEVAN and their friends, throwing their (metaphorical) black cloaks around their conspiratorial shoulders and putting on (genuine) scowls, hurried off to the vaults, or wherever they meet. "I go—I come back!" they seemed to say. And that was the first day.

Wednesday, February 17th.—When the House rose last night there were on the Order Paper one motion and seven amendments, and a curious situation developed. Mr. GREENWOOD, who leads the Labour Party and is *ex-officio* Leader of the Opposition, kept his motion on the Paper but gave his blessing to an amendment which expressed "dissatisfaction" with Sir JOHN ANDERSON's reply to the motion. On that, said the Lobbies, crisis might come, for the Beveridge Report is the touchstone of all the political future, and even the life of the Government might be in jeopardy.

So into the debate they all plunged again. It was not a very inspiring discussion, but everybody seemed deeply moved for or against the Report.

After a long time Sir KINGSLEY WOOD, the Chancellor of the Exchequer, whose fate it will (or, at least, may) be to find the gold for the new El Dorado, went to the Table to make another Government statement.

He might have contented himself with the time-honoured formula: "I have nothing to add to what my right honourable friend said yesterday." That would probably not have annoyed the House. But Sir KINGSLEY amended the formula to: "I have plenty to subtract from what my right honourable friend said yesterday," and proceeded to do quite a bit of whittling down.

The House grew angrier and angrier. Mr. ANEURIN BEVAN (just possibly with the recollection that his wife, Miss JENNIE LEE, was at that moment fighting a critical by-election in Bristol) was more explosive than ever, with Mr. SHINWELL as a sort of slow (but not too slow) match in front of him. And that was the second day.

Thursday, February 18th.—Mr. HERBERT MORRISON, no mean orator at any time, made the speech of his life to-day. The situation certainly called for it. It was a tricky job, even for him.

But he did it. The Government got through by 335 votes to 119. Whether we hear more about it or not, the local action at any rate was successful.

And that was the third day. Quite a week!

Salvage Drives

With increasingly short supplies of raw materials, salvage drives and recycling became a part of life: books were sacrificed for their paper, food waste was collected for pigs. In 1940 the press baron Lord Beaverbrook, now Minister of Aircraft Production, issued a call for the public to help build more Spitfires by donating their aluminium pots and pans. There were doubts (and still are) that those collected were ever used in manufacturing, still less the Victorian iron railings removed from Britain's parks and gardens.

"I'm afraid I must have brought in my library book."

"We're just a frying-pan short on this one."

"Business psychology, sir – we find this method produces by far the best results."

"S-a-l-v-a-g-e, Salvage – we want Salvage!"

"*Good morning! I'm your local waste-paper salvage collector.*"

"Well, if they don't come in three minutes, they'll have to storm the defences."

Our War-Time Query Corner

Ask Evangeline!

Q. Everyone seems to think we are to wear very little clothes this year. What, in your opinion, is an ideal austerity wardrobe for the well-dressed woman who would willingly put up with a little inconvenience to help to win the war? FEMINA.

A. The most austere wardrobe I can think of is the type I met once in a Frinton boarding-house, consisting of a single hook behind a curtain so arranged as to slide heavily to the floor, taking the rod with it, if one either stretched out the hand in its direction or approached it with light tread. As to the tiny garments you mention, I personally have heard nothing, but can

quite see that wee miniature undies, knee-length mackintoshes and bridal gowns, diminutive shirt-tops just long enough to tuck into the waistcoat, etc., should hold an appeal for every right-thinking man and woman as a means of beating Hitler at his own game.

*　*　*　*　*

Q. Since giving up my little Ford for the duration, I have been in the habit of bicycling to and from craft classes at our Technical Institute, where I am at present engaged on a fretwork harp-case for the lady in whom I am interested. As the institute serves in the day-time as a dormitory for

expectant mothers in the event of renewed blitzing, we craft students are forced to take our work backwards and forwards with us, no easy matter in a windy coastal resort such as this and with a framework of plywood measuring 6 ft. by 4 ft. Only last week I was twice driven out of my course—on the Wednesday afternoon into the toddlers' play-pool, on Friday evening into the constable on point duty. I need hardly add that these escapades do the harp-case no good. Can you suggest a reliable mode of piloting large objects on a pedal cycle? ENTHUSIASTIC FRETWORKER.

A. You will have to learn to tack.

This means to perform the operation of tacking or turning a vessel in a course opposite to the one in which one appears to be going; and to do so you will need a tack. Not a small, short, sharp-pointed nail, but a length of rope to confine the foremost lower corners of your instrument case, this being in the position of a stay-sail if loosely attached to a stout pole lashed to your seat on the cycle. For details on how to splice the standing jib, run up the mizzen trysail, get the reef pendant into the mainsheet block, etc., see Commander Kettle-Mess's book, *Cowes For All*, and remember that the main thing is—Hold fast to the tack (losing the tack may mean losing your seat), and keep the halyards trimmed!

*   *   *   *   *

Q. I have in my possession an envelope which, with a view to paper economy, has been passed through the post between my husband and me no fewer than twenty-seven times. Is this a record?

(Mrs.) EFFIE TIFFIN.

A. Hardly. On the advent of the twopence-ha'penny post a very old aunt of mine hit upon an even more ingenious saving scheme. She commenced sending in turn to all quarters of the Empire the same *empty unstamped* envelope. A glance at this sufficed to apprise her friends as to her continued existence, yet laid them under no obligation to redeem from the postman, and the envelope eventually returned to her home address which she kept written on the back. It now bears ninety-four postmarks, is still in circulation, and is, in fact, expected back at any moment from Blundell-sands.

*   *   *   *   *

Q. What is your opinion of the increased distances between bus-stops owing to further petrol restrictions? I have now to walk half a mile to the Blue Boar to take a mile bus-ride to the Black Bull, and even then do not always get on the bus when it comes.

OLD ETONIAN.

A. Your inability to get on the bus when it does reach the Blue Boar is surely no concern of your local transport authority's. In my opinion there is no reason why motor-buses should stop at all. Passengers wishing to alight or to board the bus could be marshalled on to a receiving platform and snatched up by swinging nets in the same way that a mail-bag is collected by an express. The nets would land them in bundles.

*   *   *   *   *

Q. Can you tell me why it is that,

though I have the sea in my veins, I have never had a proposal from a sailor? A marine once asked me to go a walk when I bumped into him in the black-out, but there has been nothing further. I am the tailor-made type of girl. Friends rave about my odd eyes, and artists have wanted to paint me for my feet alone.

(Miss) BABS HIGGINBOTTOM.

A. I know a lady at Ilfracombe who has the largest private collection of china bell-pushes in the country, yet she has never expected a proposal from the curator of the British Museum.

THE MERCHANT NAVY

FROM America comes news of further steps to share the burden of the Merchant Navy in the Battle of Supply. Remember, it is to the sacrifices of these sailors that you owe many of the comforts of civilized life which you still enjoy.

In return, will you not contribute to the PUNCH COMFORTS FUND? A gift to this Fund enables you to express your gratitude in tangible form. You owe it to our sailors to see that they are well provided with extra comforts. Donations will be gratefully received and acknowledged by Mr. Punch at PUNCH COMFORTS FUND, 10 Bouverie St., London, E.C.4.

It simply does not follow, Babs. Very likely you will find your happiness with a chiropodist or consulting optician.

*   *   *   *   *

Q. This war is getting beyond a joke when candy manufacturers of my age are forced to spend their evenings under practically arctic conditions. Since my wife's becoming leading competitor in an Inter-Suburbs Fuel-Saving Contest, not a coal has been ignited in our home, with the result that larder, box-room, cylinder cupboards and cold frames, not to mention outside offices of every type, are all utilized to house the fuel which we continue, fortnightly, to receive. This week's supply we have had to store in laundry-baskets, behind the piano in the lounge, and underneath the dining-room sofa. I have sat in overcoat, eiderdown, foot-muff and cloth cap with ear-pieces, night after night, but to no purpose. What line ought I to take? (Mr.) CLARENCE TOASTER.

A. Perhaps you have not thought of a hay-box. The entire office staff now have their own little hay-boxes, constructed and lined on the premises. All one has to do is to slip into *camera* for an odd half-hour or so when cold. We personally come out as soon as the lid begins to steam, but obviously one can lay down no rules.

*   *   *   *   *

Q. Could you suggest a suitable book present for my *fiancé* on an underground ammunition dump? He is a sanitary inspector in civil life and always likes to take an interest in his environment. (Miss) MAY CHITTY.

A. Either *Universes I Have Overlooked*—H. G. Wells, or *Our Sub-soil: Shown to the Children*, by Auntie Mavis, should be appropriate. Or if you wanted something that would keep him in touch with his peace-time occupation, what about *The Cesspool Beautiful*, by Clough Williams-Ellis and Beverley Nichols' *Quiet Moments With My Drains*?

*   *   *   *   *

Q. A new lodger, recommended to me by a traveller in wire-netting that has since been taken up by the police for something shady, is giving rise to a good bit of talk in this house on account of going up to his room regularly every afternoon, locking the door behind him, and staying there the best part of an hour making noises as can only be described as peculiar. More like mice than anything else. Do you think he is a secret agent? His window gives on to the municipal water-works and public wash-houses, which always seemed to be targets when the blitzes were on. He says he is a ship-breaker, though I have never seen him doing anything, and calls himself Eustace Pickblatt.

Mrs. BUNTY BLOSS.

A. I cannot understand anyone calling himself by the name you mention and for this reason can appreciate your feeling of mistrust. All the same there is very likely some quite simple explanation for his segregating himself in the way you describe. He may be eating his sweets ration, which would account for the sounds heard. You will notice that among sensitive folk it is becoming less and less the custom to consume anything of the chocolate variety in public. As to his being a ship-breaker—I dare say that in war-time things have to be broken up into very tiny pieces and that is the reason why you have seen no evidence of his work.

I have never heard of an agent for mice.

"Yes, I know, old man, but don't forget it's taken nearly four years of total war to get it to look like this."

"You'd better take all these old war-maps and draw the arrows going the other way round."

"Can you get me an unexpurgated copy of the Beveridge Report?"

The Children's War

Children endured all the dangers, hardships and restrictions of adults during the war, often coupled with traumatic separation from parents and broken schooling. They actively participated in the war effort, like the Boy Scout messengers of the Blitz, helping with the harvest or holding salvage drives.

"Round, and slightly flat on both ends, rather like the world. That's the best way I can describe an orange."

"Coo! Who wants conkers – we're collectin' shrapnel!"

"My husband got a load of sand and made it all just like the seaside for them."

" But you weren't always being worried to death by war talk when you were my size."

"Never mind, darlings, it's
only the guns."

"Can I have the afternoon off, Sir?
Grandma's coming home on leave."

"I got my badge for incendiary bombs all right, but I didn't
do so well with HEs."

"We teach them the three r's – reading, writing
and radiolocation."

"I understand you've been riveting in your name and address."

"Here – psst – mister – like to buy a nice golliwog or two on the quiet? Or a set o' doll's furniture? Kewpies? Toy trains? Bunnyrabbits? Cuddliedoggies? Pussinbootikins?"

"I wouldn't be seen with a civilian, only that Harold's a type that plies you with clothing coupons."

"As soon as you blokes reach the limit of human endurance we can march back for dinner."

"I remember the time when you could always flush a Heinkel there."

WAR-TIME WEAKNESSES – CUPS OF TEA.

At the Pictures

The Good Colonel

The Life and Death of Colonel Blimp (Directors: Michael Powell and Emeric Pressburger—who also produced, and wrote the story) is too long, and has a misleading title; but there is not very much else to be said against it. The title is misleading because one expects—or one would expect, if one hadn't read the notices—a more or less satirical work on the character invented and immortalized by David Low, whereas what one gets is a careful, intelligently-done and more or less serious account of the life of a conscientious, brave and not even dull-witted British Army officer whose latter-day Conservatism is little more than the common result of the inevitable hardening of by no means unusual arteries. In other words *Colonel Blimp* was always Blimp-ish even as a young man, and at any moment there are always plenty of subaltern *Blimps*; but the only trouble with *Candy*, in this story, is that he clings to the belief that right is might, that those who fight fair will win because of that fact no matter what the behaviour of their opponents. The tendency to think this is, to be sure, constitutional; but I don't think it was in the constitution of the original *Colonel Blimp*.

All the same, two hours and three-quarters is rather too much. (There seems to be no common denominator in these characters who are allowed more than a hundred and fifty minutes for their biographies: the great Ziegfeld, *Scarlett O'Hara*, *Clive Wynne-Candy*...) I don't wish to imply that the piece is not continuously entertaining: it has been done with remarkable skill and intelligence in all departments, and personally I did not dislike anything about it but the momentary piece of hokum with which it ends (that sudden, old-man's salute, slipped in to overcharge the emotional atmosphere and produce the electric crackle of applause as the picture fades). The colcur is exceedingly good and much

of the film is a pleasure for the eye, though the last-war scenes look artificial. Roger Livesey is admirable as the developing *Colonel*, Deborah Kerr skilfully differentiates between three girls who look exactly alike; and Anton Walbrook is a German so sympathetic as to have worried some of the newspapers.

Now for a picture in which Brian Donlevy, of all people, is called upon to make such weighty remarks as

[*The Life and Death of Colonel Blimp*

FACING THE CRITICAL WIND

Col. Blimp . . . . Roger Livesey

"We are faced with two different problems, each dependent upon the other"—a work which otherwise may be concisely summed up as one of those films the credit titles of which are displayed against a background of sinister shadows moving across brick walls.

For me, most of the mitigating moments in *Hangmen Also Die* (Director: Fritz Lang) were contributed by Alexander Granach, who has a fine time as the beer-drinking, bowler-hatted Gestapo Inspector *Alois Gruber*—a fruity part

indeed, and brilliantly done. There is some other excellent small-part playing which livens up a few of the sequences we know so well; and the straight-forward "chase" part of the story is as effective as a well-directed man-hunt always is—more so than usual, in fact, since the man-hunt is Mr. Lang's directorial speciality and by this time he knows how to get more out of it than anyone else. But I don't take much pleasure in this kind of film: the constant insistence upon brutality—the *details* of brutality—sours the whole thing.

For a lesson in the way this kind of story should be told, see the Crown Film Unit's *The Silent Village* (Director: Humphrey Jennings), which, basically about the same thing, manages to be ten times as moving, impressive and memorable in a quarter the length. This, too, is about the murder of Heydrich; but it has the sense to understate instead of underlining. The mining village of Cwmgiedd acts as the mining village of Lidice, and we see what would have happened in Wales very much as it did happen in Czechoslovakia. There are no professional actors: these are all the people of the Swansea and Dulais valleys. The sense of brutal oppression is there, the misery and resentment of the people under it is no less faithfully conveyed than in the Lang film; but it is done without any of the Lang film's smart, monocled, jack-booted toughs, without any of the Lang film's careful and obvious and detailed (and familiar) displays of exactly what *sort* of violence and intellectual and physical torment the Nazi oppressors employ. In my view this makes the short Jennings picture better than the long Lang picture; though not, of course, in the view of the expectant queues outside the Tivoli.

Another comparatively short film must have a word here: Paul Rotha's documentary *World of Plenty*, which runs for nearly an hour and is about the problem of food distribution. It is stimulating, informative and a first-rate basis for discussion.   R. M.

"By the way, I managed to get some corned beef for dinner."

"Actually, the Russians driving on Rostov are on just now. By the time you get your ticket there'll be the Japs in Rabaul, and by the time you sit down there'll be Donald Duck."

In Which We Serve:

SPEECH DAYS IN THE SILENT SERVICE.

Captain 'D':. . . . . Noel Coward

What's on the Wireless?

Listening to the BBC Home Service on the radio became a national habit, essential for up-to-the-minute war news at nine o'clock, the latest government information and some welcome entertainment.

"We've a few minutes in hand before the news – how about going over some of the old Russian place-names together."

"It's no use turning on the news now: the worst is over."

"Well, that is the end of 'Works Wonders', so back to work we go."

"Just turned nine – what's on the wireless, dear?"

BEAU GESTE

"Three cheers for the star-spangled tricolor!
Three cheers for the Red, White and Blue!"

"ACCORDING TO PLAN"

ON THE QUAY-SIDE

"So much for Africa. Now for the next Continent."

THE SONG OF THE RUHR

(General Dwight Eisenhower leads the successful Allied invasion of
North Africa and, with General Alexander, plans a European front. The
Red Army wins victory after victory, while Allied bombing of the Ruhr
devastates Germany's industrial heartland.)

THE FATES DECIDE.

(At the Third Washington Conference, Churchill, Roosevelt and Stalin
plan the Italian Campaign and the continued bombing of Germany.)

"Right-o, I'll tell you what I'll do: I'll swap our second piano-tuner for one of your six comedians if you'll give me a written guarantee that he isn't a female impersonator."

"Cor! Someone ain't 'arf goin' ter cop a packet tonight, mate. They are ours, ain't they?"

No. 5338   PUNCH SUMMER NUMBER—June 7 1943   Volume CCV

PUNCH

SUMMER 1 NUMBER

Impressions of Parliament

Business Done

Tuesday, September 21st.—House of Commons: Churchill's History of the War—the Greatest Chapter so Far.

Tuesday, September 21st.—An audience and a setting that even the haughtiest of opera stars would have delighted in awaited the reappearance of the Grand Story-teller of Britain when he re-entered the House ' of Commons to-day to give some more chapters of his History of the Great War.

Brigadier CHARLES HOWARD, the Serjeant at Arms, whose unenviable task it is to find seats for "strangers" who want to listen to the debates, seems to be able to get more and more people into the strictly limited accommodation available. Peers scrambled into queer odd corners of the carved panelling. Ambassadors—including the United States' JOHN WINANT—sat squeezed into a solid row. Lord MARGESSON, first on the scene (as becomes a former Government Chief Whip), was soon surrounded by other members of Another Place.

Mr. DONALD NELSON, President ROOSEVELT's supply go-getter, was there too, piloted by Captain SOMERSET DE CHAIR, M.P., who is in the British Ministry of Production. Opposite, wearing a black and red snood, was Mrs. CHURCHILL, with a lot more peers standing and sitting around her.

Down on the floor M.P.s draped themselves in places never intended as seats for mortal man. Ministers were well content to find standing-room in remote parts of the Chamber. And all talked loudly and uninterruptedly through the Question-hour which led up to the entry of the Prime Minister.

Mr. CHURCHILL had a score of questions down for answer, but was not there in time, so the Speaker announced that they would be put off, in a block, until later in the week. Nobody murmured. Then Mr. EDEN, leading the House, suggested that, as the Prime Minister's speech would have to be a long one, there should be a lunch interval half way. Just as the House was silently assenting to this unusual plan there was a roar of cheers, and Members looked as if they had received the order: "Eyes right!" —or "left!"—as every gaze was turned towards the door behind the Speaker's Chair.

Round that ornate symbol strolled

THE WORLD

A PANORAMA

"Let observation with extensive view Survey the war from China to Peru."

Mr. CHURCHILL, looking more like his caricatures than ever, and lacking only the cigar. Very slowly he walked down the row of hastily-retracted feet in front of the Treasury Bench and, bowing, sat down while Mr. EDEN had a brief "barge" with other Members over the lunch-time adjournment plan.

Then up he got with an enormous pile of notes in his hands, to plunge at once into his story. And *what* a story! The Local Boy had certainly Made Good, for it was an almost unbroken tale of success. The R.A.F. was dropping in Germany now three times as many bombs as it was last year, with lower losses. And the R.A.F. alone had fifty per cent. more planes in action than Germany. We could speedily increase our air force— the Germans could not make theirs grow so fast. That opened prospects of saturating Germany's defences, with results that might in themselves be decisive of the fate of the world.

HITLER might—*might*—have a secret weapon, but if he had we should probably find the answer, the antidote, to it. We had lost no merchant ship in the North Atlantic for four months. But (Mr. CHURCHILL ostentatiously touched the wood of the Table) he could give no guarantee that that good fortune would continue, for hordes of U-boats were out again, *and at that moment were attacking a convoy in the Atlantic.*

This piece of news, slipped in quite casually, startled the House, and brought home to it in a blinding flash of realism the grim truth of Mr. CHURCHILL's comment that the war was not over yet, well as it was going.

That, indeed, was the theme of his speech: All is going well—BUT victory,

now perhaps within our sight, can come within our grasp only if we all co-operate and work for it.

Over and over again he repeated the warning in various words and settings.

There was a graceful and grateful tribute to the officers and men of the Merchant Navy, "on whom the nation never calls in vain," a joke about the Japanese, who once fought to the last man but who now seemed to prefer retirement and continued life to the glory of a fighting end on the battle-field — even though we were pre-pared to offer every assistance in the maintenance of the age-old Japanese tradition.

Mr. CHURCHILL told the story of the Italian armistice—how an Italian General had pleaded with our Ambas-sadors in Madrid and Lisbon for an end to the war, had been told that the only terms were unconditional sur-render, and had accepted gladly.

The Premier exclaimed: "Critics say forty days were unnecessarily lost to our military plans while we negotiated this armistice! Not *one* day was lost —not *one*: not one *moment*!"

Leaning fiercely over the table, Mr. CHURCHILL rapped: "When I hear talk of throwing armies on this and that beach, I marvel at the lack of know-ledge by our critics about modern warfare "

We had been generous with Italy, he went on, because we felt that she had been misled, but with Germany (his voice hardened and his jaw set) the case was different, because twice in our life-time Germany had plunged the world into war, and Prussian militarism and Nazi tyranny must both go before there could be talk of peace.

By this time, in spite of the promise of a feeding interval, M.P.s were making a somewhat noisy rush for what Mr. ARTHUR GREENWOOD called a "little sustenance," and Mr. CHURCHILL suspended his remarkable one-man drama for an hour.

On the resumption, as the football reporters say, Mr. CHURCHILL went on to tell the story of the invasion of Italy by the Allies, and got a cheer for the announcement that the latest reports showed that the enemy was "worsted." He plunged into an account of the military steps taken, and, turning suddenly to the Opposition, demanded: *"Is that all right?"*

When the military advisers thought the time ripe we should invade the West of Europe, and the bloodiest of our trials was perhaps yet to come. Thus ended perhaps the most thrill-ing instalment (so far) of Churchill's History of the Great War.

THE TIRED TOURIST

"If you go to the South of Italy you'll find nothing but British and Americans. The season's over for Corsica, and you wouldn't care for Elba, I suppose."

(On September 29, the Italian Army under Marshal Badoglio signed an armistice with the Allies. Here, German Foreign Minister Joachim von Ribbentrop advises Mussolini on his next move.)

"I don't mind telling you that this offence is punishable with penal servitude, or even death, but in view of your inexperience I shall just admonish you and fine you the sum of ninepence."

"There's some talk now of Lord Woolton putting eggs in shells."

"Sorry, Guv'nor; but if I was to take everyone wot wants me I shouldn't 'ave no petrol left for cruisin' around."

Bevin Boys

After the mistaken conscription of skilled miners into the armed forces, by December 1943 coal supplies were dangerously low: manpower to produce more was urgently needed. Bevin Boys – nicknamed after Ernest Bevin, the Minister of Labour and National Service – were the randomly chosen conscripts sent to carry out their National Service in the mines rather than the military. Receiving none of the benefits due to servicemen, there was little recognition of their contribution to the war effort until recently. Famous former Bevin Boys include comedian Eric Morecambe and playwright Peter Shaffer.

"Yes, I quite see that if only I had wrapped the pipes with all the old clothes and blankets I haven't got, and kept up a roaring fire with all the coal I can't get, I shouldn't now be telephoning for the plumber that can't come."

"Oh, Mr Gimbel, would you mind settling an argument?"

"But you're mistaken, dear – it's our night for sharing your fire!"

THE BATTLE FRONT

"Down, lads, and at 'em!"

"And another thing – if someone asks you for
a cup of tea, a razor-blade and a packet of
envelopes, don't start worrying your head trying
to find some logical connection between them."

"He's got some lovely kippers under the counter, but don't go saying I told
you. Just tell him you heard from an inspired source."

"Now that we know we
are going to win I think it
much better not to be TOO
optimistic."

"No, you CAN'T have it for salvage. I want it to jump
on in Piccadilly when peace comes!"

" Hey – taxi!"

A Summer Morning on the London Road. 1843.

—and 1943.

1944

THE GREAT ENDEAVOUR

"Get a direct hit on this building and you knock the whole of their filing system on the head."

"Start off with, say a saturation raid on Kiel and then lead up to the float chamber sprocket of our Bigley carburettor."

"Which Sergeant Edwards do you wish to speak to?"

THE LISTENER

"Come along, get moving, there's nothing difficult about it – I'm not asking you to do anything that I haven't done."

"Now, have you each got YOUR identity card, in case someone in there starts getting technical?"

"They say, can we do two hundred and eighty-seven Dainty Afternoon Teas?"

"I've been drafted to joint operations, Sir – am I at the right place?"

PUNCH almanack 1944

"The ironic part is that it's no change for me — I used to come here every year."

January	**February**	**March**	**April**	**May**	**June**
S .2 . 9 . 16 . 23 . 30	S . . . 6 . 13 . 20 . 27	S . . . 5 . 12 . 19 . 26	S .2 . 9 . 16 . 23 . 30	S . . . 7 . 14 . 21 . 28	S . . . 4 . 11 . 18 . 25
M .3 . 10 . 17 . 24 . 31	M . . . 7 . 14 . 21 . 28	M . . . 6 . 13 . 20 . 27	M .3 . 10 . 17 . 24 . . .	M .1 . 8 . 15 . 22 . 29	M . . . 5 . 12 . 19 . 26
Tu .4 . 11 . 18 . 25 . . .	Tu .1 . 8 . 15 . 22 . 29	Tu . . . 7 . 14 . 21 . 28	Tu .4 . 11 . 18 . 25 . . .	Tu .2 . 9 . 16 . 23 . 30	Tu . . . 6 . 13 . 20 . 27
W .5 . 12 . 19 . 26 . . .	W . . . 2 . 9 . 16 . 23 . . .	W .1 . 8 . 15 . 22 . 29	W .5 . 12 . 19 . 26 . . .	W . . . 3 . 10 . 17 . 24 . 31	W . . . 7 . 14 . 21 . 28
Th .6 . 13 . 20 . 27 . . .	Th . 3 . 10 . 17 . 24 . . .	Th .2 . 9 . 16 . 23 . 30	Th .6 . 13 . 20 . 27 . . .	Th .4 . 11 . 18 . 25 . . .	Th .1 . 8 . 15 . 22 . 29
F .7 . 14 . 21 . 28 . . .	F . 4 . 11 . 18 . 25 . . .	F . 3 . 10 . 17 . 24 . 31	F .7 . 14 . 21 . 28 . . .	F .5 . 12 . 19 . 26 . . .	F .2 . 9 . 16 . 23 . 30
S 1 . 8 . 15 . 22 . 29 . . .	S . 5 . 12 . 19 . 26 . . .	S . 4 . 11 . 18 . 25 . . .	S 1 . 8 . 15 . 22 . 29 . . .	S .6 . 13 . 20 . 27 . . .	S . 3 . 10 . 17 . 24 . . .
July	**August**	**September**	**October**	**November**	**December**
S .2 . 9 . 16 . 23 . 30	S . . . 6 . 13 . 20 . 27	S . . . 3 . 10 . 17 . 24	S .1 . 8 . 15 . 22 . 29	S . . . 5 . 12 . 19 . 26	S . . . 3 . 10 . 17 . 24 . 31
M .3 . 10 . 17 . 24 . 31	M . . . 7 . 14 . 21 . 28	M . . . 4 . 11 . 18 . 25	M .2 . 9 . 16 . 23 . 30	M . . . 6 . 13 . 20 . 27	M .4 . 11 . 18 . 25 . . .
Tu .4 . 11 . 18 . 25 . . .	Tu .1 . 8 . 15 . 22 . 29	Tu . . . 5 . 12 . 19 . 26	Tu .3 . 10 . 17 . 24 . 31	Tu . . . 7 . 14 . 21 . 28	Tu .5 . 12 . 19 . 26 . . .
W .5 . 12 . 19 . 26 . . .	W . . . 2 . 9 . 16 . 23 . 30	W . . . 6 . 13 . 20 . 27	W .4 . 11 . 18 . 25 . . .	W .1 . 8 . 15 . 22 . 29	W .6 . 13 . 20 . 27 . . .
Th .6 . 13 . 20 . 27 . . .	Th . 3 . 10 . 17 . 24 . 31	Th . . . 7 . 14 . 21 . 28	Th .5 . 12 . 19 . 26 . . .	Th .2 . 9 . 16 . 23 . 30	Th .7 . 14 . 21 . 28 . . .
F .7 . 14 . 21 . 28 . . .	F . 4 . 11 . 18 . 25 . . .	F .1 . 8 . 15 . 22 . 29	F . 6 . 13 . 20 . 27 . . .	F . 3 . 10 . 17 . 24 . . .	F 1 . 8 . 15 . 22 . 29 . . .
S 1 . 8 . 15 . 22 . 29 . . .	S . 5 . 12 . 19 . 26 . . .	S .2 . 9 . 16 . 23 . 30	S . 7 . 14 . 21 . 28 . . .	S . 4 . 11 . 18 . 25 . . .	S 2 . 9 . 16 . 23 . 30 . . .

"I'd have stopped him in 1936, wouldn't you?"

"I'm the company's official war artist."

"I don't know what we should have done without you, Sir. Do you mind if I have your fare?"

"During alerts we dispense with the cover charge."

"Look here, I wish you'd go to the main entrance. It's only a couple of hundred yards down the road, and it'd save me all the bother of shooting you."

"...then I know by the length of Timothy's lead if we're at the station."

"*And this time next year what will they say?   It'll be 'Improve on whatever you done last year.'*"

Down on the Farm

Even before the start of the war, the Ministry of Agriculture had encouraged farmers to turn more acreage over to food production – Britain needed to be able to feed itself during the conflict. As the war went on pressure increased, along with the paperwork.

"Yes – Farmer Giles speaking."

"What do you want us to do now!"

"Stockman, tractor-driver, hedge-layer – h'm – how's your Italian?"

"My nephew's expecting to invade the Continent very shortly."

"Is there any significance in the fact that the pork sausage is crossed out rather more heavily than the meat pie?"

"At present I'm in the old 23 Laburnum Park Road, SW5, but she's overdue for a refit, so I might find myself on the beach at any moment."

"If you want my opinion, Sir, it won't be long before they're taking down all them window-boards and putting them up again for the peace-night celebrations."

"We'll 'ave this little job fixed for you in no time, Mum – my mate's got an appointment for an 'air-do!"

"You'll have to do something to this room to match your Utility furniture."

Impressions of Parliament

Business Done

Tuesday, June 6th.—House of Commons: THE DAY—D DAY.

Wednesday, June 7th.—House of Commons: Location of Industry.

Thursday, June 8th.—House of Commons: Almost a Statement.

Tuesday, June 6th.—Was there a Member of the House of Commons who to-day did not have the mental "flash-back" beloved of the Hollywood producer?

Almost precisely four years ago, Mr. WINSTON CHURCHILL, grim-faced but resolute, stood at the dispatch box in the old House of Commons —now, alas! itself a victim of the *Luftwaffe*—and proclaimed to an impressed if sceptical world that Britain would "fight on the beaches . . . in the streets . . . in the fields . . . but would NEVER give in."

At first light this morning parachutists swooped, landing barges crept inshore, warplanes filled the skies, warships poured a hail of shells into the shore batteries.

But they were *our* parachutists, *our* landing - barges, *our* warships, *our* shells. They were attacking and pounding *their* beaches. It was D Day.

Again the House of Commons was filled by excited Members, waiting to hear the Prime Minister speak. The Day for which the world had waited for many weary months had dawned, and Mr. CHURCHILL was to tell the first story, as he alone can tell a story.

He was not there. Questions were ploughed through. Nobody wanted to listen to them, but fair-play is fair-play, free speech is free speech, and so the entire House sat (more or less) silent, its eyes on the door, its ears unheeding, its thoughts . . . far away on the shores of France, with the dauntless men of the Allied forces.

At length, even the ingenuity of supplementary question-askers failed, and (in spite of a spirited last-question stand by Mr. WILLIAM MABANE, of the Ministry of Food) question-time was over. There was a pause. Mr. ANTHONY EDEN, Leader of the House, looked inquiringly at the door. Mr. CLEM ATTLEE, the Deputy Prime Minister, leaned forward—and looked at the door. Brigadier HARVIE WATT, the Prime Minister's tireless Parliamentary Private Secretary, not only looked at,

but made for the door. The Government Chief Whip, Mr. JAMES STUART, stepped swiftly up to the SPEAKER'S Chair, conferred in a whisper with Mr. Speaker.

"There must," Mr. Speaker announced, "be a short interval before the Prime Minister arrives."

It was as though he had switched on a particularly loud loud-speaker, for the entire House began to talk excitedly at once. Mr. EDEN sprinted across the floor and sat on the steps by the side of Mr. LLOYD GEORGE, who had had to make so many historic pronouncements when he led the nation in that other war which now seems so long ago.

Suddenly the door swung open and into the Chamber walked a familiar

TIME'S REVENGE

figure, three typewritten sheets in his hands. There was a second of dead silence as everybody who could looked at the expressive face of the Prime Minister. From his expression much can be gleaned by the knowing. What they saw aroused a roar almost of triumph—a roar that spread speedily round the Chamber.

Skilfully stepping over the feet of his Ministers, Mr. CHURCHILL arrived at the dispatch box, leaned on it, and— began an account of the long campaign that had led only forty-eight hours earlier to the capture of Rome from the Germans—"a glorious event," he called it. Was there to be nothing of D Day, of the great events by the side of which even the liberation of Rome paled?

With the little smile that creeps unbidden to his lips when he is indulging in a gentle pull of the

House's collective leg, Mr. CHURCHILL turned very slowly to his third typed sheet, and the silence that had seemed complete became more intense.

"I have to announce to the House," said he quietly, "that during the night the first of a series of landings in force upon the European Continent has taken place."

The House roared a breathless cheer, cut it short, strained for the next words.

So the House of Commons heard the news of what may perhaps be the greatest, the most significant event it has ever known.

"Thus far the commanders who are engaged report that everything is proceeding according to plan—and *what* a plan!" said Mr. CHURCHILL, and this time the House stopped him dead with a full-throated roar of cheers.

Waiting for silence, Mr. CHURCHILL remarked in almost matter-of-fact tones that nothing that equipment, science or forethought could do had been neglected, that the ardour and spirit of the troops was splendid to witness.

Again the cheers crashed.

Æons ago—on September 2 1939, to be precise—Mr. ARTHUR GREENWOOD, then leading the Opposition, was exhorted by parts of an excited and slightly hysterical House to "speak for England." To-day, if never before, he did so. In a low voice he said:

"There is nothing that *we* can do except perhaps to pledge our physical and spiritual resources to the unstinted aid of the men and women who are serving overseas, and to let them know the pride that we shall feel in their victories, the sadness we shall feel about their losses. Will the Prime Minister report frequently to Parliament, so that we may, on the one hand, share such tribulations as may come and, on the other hand, take joy in achievement?"

A moment Mr. CHURCHILL sat still. The House was silent, moved beyond measure. Then there was a great husky cheer, in tribute to as simply and finely-expressed a sentiment as any ever heard in the House. Mr. CHURCHILL promised, then hurried off.

The House talked about the Colonies, but its heart was not in the discussion.

At the end of the day, the benches filled up again, and into the Chamber, with confident, springy step, came Mr. CHURCHILL once more.

All was going well, said he, and our

"It's quite an enjoyable book, if you're prepared to skip the chapters describing how the war ended in 1942."

losses were much less—"*very* much less," he repeated with heavy emphasis —than had been expected. Obstacles that had been expected to be formidable were now "behind us." And all continued to go well.

Wednesday, June 7th.—It was Mr. ANTHONY EDEN, with his gift for the right phrase, who to-day provided the epilogue to yesterday's thrilling news. Answering a question, Mr. EDEN spoke of "The forthcoming victory of the United Nations."

It was so uncompromising, so unquestioned, so flat, that it roused a great cheer. As if relieved from the intolerable strain of suspense waiting for D Day had involved, the House was in almost jovial mood to-day.

Lest history forget (or perchance even overlook) them, your scribe records with respectful pen these pearls of the political thinker's art casually cast this day before . . . before fellow-legislators:

"Very few people now travel for fun."—Mr. NOEL-BAKER, Ministry of War Transport.

"Will the Government consider reducing the turnip content in our jam?"—Colonel GREENWELL.

"May we have more prunes?"— Captain PLUGGE.

"In the spring a lady's fancy lightly turns to thoughts of hats."—Sir ARCHIBALD SOUTHBY.

"Is it in order to describe the records of Members of this House as 'muck-raking'?"—Mr. SILVERMAN.

Perhaps the last verbal jewel may be amplified—or polished. It arose (as they say in supplementary questions) out of a comment made by Mr. BEVERLEY BAXTER—who seemed to be annoyed about something—on a recent book called *Your M.P.*, which "made remarks" about quite a lot of Conservative M.P.s and their records, while maintaining a discreet silence about those of other political persuasions. The publisher, said Mr. BAXTER tartly, was a "muck-raker."

At once Mr. SILVERMAN intervened with his query, to which Mr. Speaker replied that it was "a matter of taste."

Mr. BRACKEN, who had not been careful to conceal his dislike of the book and its unknown author, added (to loud non-Party cheers) the opinion that it was a pity strained stocks of paper were used to lower the reputation of the House at a time when the greatest military operations in history were beginning.

Mr. SHINWELL protested with some heat at this comment, to be told

briskly that he was "in too much of a hurry to become an elder statesman." Mr. SHINWELL's protests grew louder, more vehement, and he was told soothingly by Mr. Speaker that all had to take the rough with the smooth.

Everybody looked hopefully around when Questions ended, but Mr. CHURCHILL's seat remained empty, so Members began to debate on the location of industry, which was the subject of the Barlow (or was it Beveridge, Uthwatt or Scott?) report.

It seems that the Government is going to do something about the location of industry—when there *is* some industry and "locations" are less needed by the devotees of that essential if not exactly productive, industry: national defence.

Thursday, June 8th.—Mr. CHURCHILL turned up to-day, and M.P.s craned forward eagerly to listen to his expected war-statement.

He gave it. It was simply to the effect that, while maintaining public morale (if that were needed), Members should sound a note of caution to their constituents, and try to ensure that optimism was restrained. For, while great dangers lay behind us, great exertions lay before us.

It was a timely reminder.

"Now you know why I always went Calais-Dover."

"You want to ask 'im about when ole Jerry was 'ere – you won't 'arf 'ear some irregular verbs."

"If we hurry we should be able to capture it in time for the nine o'clock news."

"German planeless pilots they are, lady."

*"Civilization at last, Mr Harrington – do you see the
balloon barrage ahead?"*

*"Only about one in a thousand shows the
slightest signs of individuality."*

" No, Albert, you mustn't talk to Mum now ! "

D Day in Our Suburb

DDAY passed off fairly quietly in our suburb. But there was a lot of talk.

Saltby said: "This thing has taken me by surprise. All the indications were that the 8th would be the day." Asked "What indications?" he opened his mouth pretty wide, said "Well——" and closed it again very tightly, with the air of a man who but for over-riding considerations of national security could have made some remarkably interesting disclosures.

This impressed nobody, since everyone knows, Mrs. Saltby being a great talker with few reticences, that Saltby decides almost every point of importance by a process of counting on his way home from the station in the evenings. Thus he may tell himself that if he sees a black cat before he has counted up to two hundred, Invasion Day will be before the middle of June, or he may decide that if he has counted up to two hundred black cats before he gets home he will refrain from putting his tomatoes out for another week; this according to Mrs. Saltby, who adds, regrettably, "the great baby." We do not altogether despise Saltby for this habit, being perhaps not above a little counting ourselves, but we take his wisdom after the event for what it is worth.

Meadows said, on the morning of June 6th, "This isn't the real thing of course. Merely a feint," and he has been saying it ever since. A knowledge of Meadows tells us that he will go on saying it, if necessary, right up to the gates of Berlin. He says he knows where the real blow is coming and is even prepared to lay his finger on the map and say "There!"—provided Earle isn't about of course. Earle, according to Meadows, is a talker and not to be trusted to keep anything to himself for half an hour. "Remember that exercise?" Meadows says, and that is the end of Earle as far as he is concerned.

This is rather bad luck on Earle, whose only offence was to say to a member of the opposing platoon, on the morning of a Home Guard exercise, that whatever happened he proposed to finish up at the "Three Horses." This, since that famous inn was in fact our objective, was said to have given away the direction of our attack. If so, as Earle pointed out, he ought to have been praised for misleading the enemy, since on account of the darkness and a certain inexperience in those days, our attack actually took quite a different direction and ended with the capture unopposed of old Lady Throttle's greenhouses.

At a later stage in the war it may be possible to tell the full story of that night's work. For the moment it must be enough to say that the problem of fighting in greenhouses is not adequately covered in the text-books. A man who runs into a nest of potted geraniums in the dark may easily find himself in serious difficulties.

However, we were talking about D Day.

A man with the unusual name of Haybottle observed last night in the "Three Horses" that it was all rot this talk of dropping 60-ton tanks behind the German lines by parachute. As nobody had suggested such a thing we let this go, but when Haybottle said darkly that as a matter of fact they were doing much more remarkable things than that, we were constrained to ask him "What things?" He said "Ah!" and explained that he had a brother in a minesweeper who knew all about it but was closer than an oyster. "In that case," we said, "how do you know about these remarkable things we are doing?"

"I don't," he said.

"Then how do you know we *are* doing any remarkable things?" asked Saltby.

"Well, aren't we?" said Haybottle.

Everyone had to agree that we were, but there was a general feeling that we had in some way been tricked out of this argument. Before long Saltby was at him again.

"This cousin of yours on the minelayer——" he began.

"Brother in a mine*sweeper*," said Haybottle.

"Never mind that," said Saltby, annoyed. "I suppose he was over there on D Day, was he?"

"Right in the thick of it."

"Seen him since?"

"Hardly likely, is it," said Haybottle loftily, "that he'd have time to drop in here for a bitter in the intervals of sweeping? Some of you chaps seem to have extraordinary ideas about the Navy."

"In that case," said Saltby, jumping in for the kill, "how do you know he was there on D Day?"

"I saw him," said Haybottle.

"*You* saw him!" cried Meadows. "What on earth were *you* doing there?"

"Don't tell me we sent in a troop of Shock Solicitors with the first wave," said Saltby.

"Tell us all about it," said Earle eagerly.

"Not allowed to," said Haybottle, draining his glass and, it being his turn to pay, walking swiftly from the bar.

"Well," said Saltby slowly, "what do you know about that?"

None of us, as usual, knew anything, but we managed to talk about it for three quarters of an hour.

"Anyway, it'll be in all the papers to-morrow," said Meadows finally.

"What makes you think that?" we asked.

"Ask Earle," said Meadows. H. F. E.

"Didn't I tell you it would start on the sixth?"

"He refuses to confess where he bought the elastic."

How much
WASTE PAPER
have you put out this week? Remember how badly it is needed, and try to find more.

" ... and make an extra copy for the Wastepaper Salvage Committee."

"Why's that lady blacked-out, Daddy?"

"I say – what a persuasive man."

LIBERATION

"They're coming!"

THE ISLAND-SPEARER

(US General Douglas Macarthur battles his way across the Pacific towards Japan.)

The Brains Trust

The Brains Trust was first broadcast on January 1, 1941 (initially as *Any Questions*) after demand from radio listeners for more educational fare. With its panel of experts – regulars and guests – answering questions on topics from the irreverent to the erudite, *The Brains Trust* became one of Britain's most popular radio programmes, receiving around 4,000 questions a week at its peak. Questions on religion and politics were banned and the panel was frequently accused of left-wing bias.

"But, darling, perhaps there won't be any Brains Trust *when you grow up."*

"Anybody want The Brains Trust*?"*

"Four listeners submitted all-correct solutions and each will receive a cheque for £62 10s. Here are their names: J Huxley, CEM Joad, AB Campbell and RT Gould."

THE BRAINS TRUST:

BRAINS AT WORK.
Commander Campbell, Miss Jennie Lee, Donald McCullough, Colonel Walter Elliot, Dr CEM Joad, Dr Julian Huxley

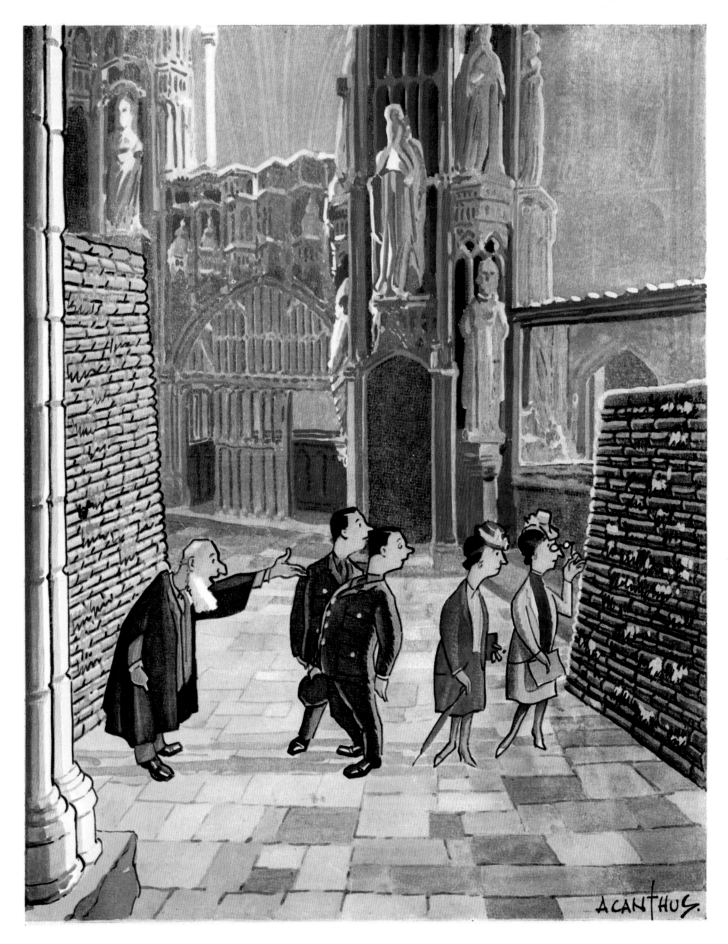

"*For 15th Century it's in good repair—but the sandbags need restoration.*"

"Of course, after the war we shall go back to clothes-pegs."

*"I'm afraid business conditions won't allow us to raise your salary, Miss
Simpson, but as a slight token of their esteem the directors have decided to
present you with all their personal sweet coupons."*

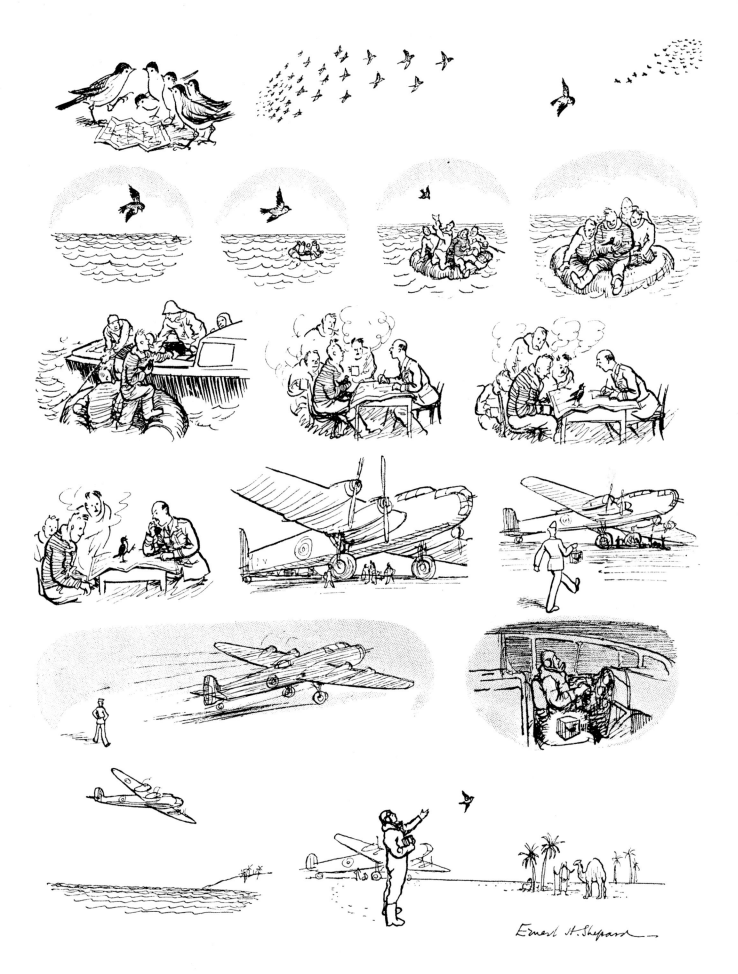

THE MIGRANT

" Good morning, madam—and what can't I show you? "

An Industrial Case-Book

(Written in collaboration with the Welfare and Industrial Relations Officer of the Snacker and Diplocket Small Things Co. (1928), Ltd.)

I

FROM ——, —— and Sons, Ltd., comes a request for guidance in the administration and organization of crèches. The spate of reports and blueprints on educational reform has somehow made the workers of the company hypercritical of existing services. It is said, for example, that the curriculum of our crèche is hopelessly inadequate and positively anti-social. At a recent meeting of the Workers' Welfare Society a crane-operator, Morgan Thomas, delivered a vitriolic address in which he analysed the activities of the infants and tried to prove that their training was purely vocational.

"It is the old, old story," he said. "The capitalist usurers have seen the writing on the wall: they know that changes are imminent and they seek to safeguard their further supplies of semi-skilled manual labour by moulding the minds of our children to their own selfish designs. Can they deny that jig-saw games are merely a form of specialized training for machine-tool assembly? Can they deny that peg-fitting and 'Turn-a-ball, Mary,' lead to blind-alley occupations?"

We have passed the letter on to Mr. Butler.

II

"Can you tell us where we can obtain the sheet-music of the new national anthem of our Russian Allies?" writes the Industrial Relations Officer of the Empty Box (Corrugated) Co., Ltd. "Our operatives are getting very restive and assign the basest motives to our genuine inability to furnish the works' band with the complete score. Do you think we should do better to write direct to Moscow?"

III

"Tell me," writes the General Manager of Snacker and Diplocket, Ltd., "where is rumour bred? In the packing-shop or in the foundry? We *have* had our hands full these last few weeks and no mistake. Talk about discontent! In swift succession amazing rumours (all of them completely unfounded, of course) have swept through the works.

The canteen tea is being doctored with harmful stimulants in an effort to lash us into a frenzy of production for the Second Front. This was the first assault of the whispering campaign. Within twenty-four hours the mythical drugs had been identified as heroin, trioxybenzamethylophosasalacylica, and tannin. Output has not, so far, suffered in the least, but the management is gravely concerned about the future. Faced with seemingly insoluble problems of reconstruction the directors were looking to the catering side of the business to recover losses on production. If the workers persist in boycotting the canteen after the war the outlook will be black indeed.

Workers who have directors billeted on them are having their faith in the working-class movement steadily undermined. It is said, for example, that aspidistras are disappearing from bow-windows, that aitches are being dropped, that the off-licence business at 'The Four Horse-Shoes' is improving at the expense of the turnover in the tap-room, and that absenteeism due to gout is on the increase. The wickedness of these falsehoods is very apparent when it is remembered that every director of the company has at some time or another spoken warmly of many of the Beveridge proposals, and has even advocated the drafting of a bill to give effect to some of them—in a modified form, of course.

The slogans and messages that we patriotic workers chalk on our bombs are paled into insignificance by the advertisements stencilled across them by Mr. Diplocket. Rumour number three originates from the hysterical chatter of a castings-fettler, Miss Eunice Moot. She claims that her brother, in Italy, has actually handled bombs marked 'BOMBS BY SNACKER AND DIPLOCKET MADE THIS WAR POSSIBLE.'

Mr. Diplocket has challenged any worker to produce a bomb so marked, and has expressed his willingness to submit the case to a handwriting expert. The rumour, however, continues to circulate in an anti-clockwise direction."

"Purely from a publicity point of view, the necessity for camouflage suits us very well."

"Time, gentlemen, please."

"Hark – a buzz bomb."
" I can't hear a thing."
"Then it must be a rocket."

"No, Doris, the point is that it goes so fast that first of
all you hear the bang as it hits the ground, and then
you hear the rumble as it flies through the air..." "Ah
– and finally, I suppose, you hear the squeak as they fill
their fountain-pens and start to invent the nasty thing!"

"No, I know this one dropped on Thursday, dear, because
that was the day Auntie Mabel's canary got out."

"There's a rumour that clothes rationing's ended – we'd all better hurry and use up our coupons."

"Mr Goddard is fighting in the Burmese jungle – perhaps you would prefer to see Mr Wright."

"Wouldn't it be marvellous if the war ended on Guy Fawkes night?"

"And as for your wife, I think we can put a lot of it down to war weariness."

"Paging Private Watson. Paging Private Watson . . ."

221

The Post-War World

Planning for a better post-war world began long before the end of the war, with the appearance of groundbreaking proposals like the Beveridge Report of 1942 – the foundations of the welfare state – and the Abercrombie Plans of 1943 and 1944 for the reconstruction of London. Meanwhile, many longed simply for a return to normal life and their old job.

"He's the chap in the Post-War Planning Section who keeps rushing in and out borrowing my rubber."

"What was the post-war world like after the last war?"

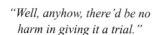

"Well, anyhow, there'd be no harm in giving it a trial."

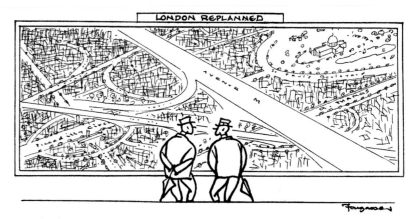

"As you see, Peabody, your old job is still waiting for you."

"That's Gilchrist—in charge of post-war planning."

FULL CIRCLE
"Isn't this where we came in?"

THE HOME-COMING

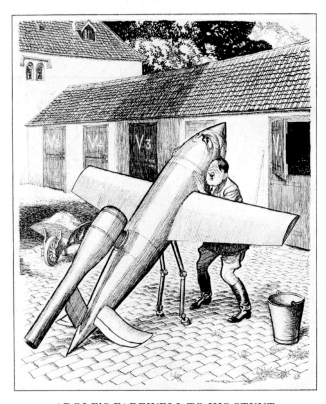

ADOLF'S FAREWELL TO HIS STUNT
*"The time may be at hand when we two must part;
but it's been wonderful while it lasted."*

THE DEBT
*"Never before has so much been owed by so many to
so few."*

(Stalin's ambitions in Eastern Europe became clear, while a new Housing Act aimed to provide
300,000 prefabricated homes. Autumn saw Allied forces overrun German V-1 flying bomb
bases and Hitler, Goebbels and Himmler cower before the peoples of occupied Europe.)

FROM WEST TO EAST

"I looks towards you."

1945

Paths to Victory

"The old place hasn't changed a bit from 1917!"

"I don't know who he is – the children brought him back from their evacuation village."

"This week's subject for discussion is 'The World I Want After the War.' Would someone please prod Gunner Tomkins sharply in the ribs and ask him what sort of world he wants after the war."

TROUBLE WITH SOME OF THE PIECES

(Churchill, Roosevelt and Stalin met at Yalta to discuss the re-organisation
of post-war Europe. It was here Stalin's plans for Poland became apparent.)

"Have you ever stopped to think that if it wasn't for Hitler we might never have been lance-corporals?"

"How soon are they getting married?" *"Well – she's got her icing-sugar."*

"You remember my telling you all about my job last month? Well, it's no longer hush-hush."

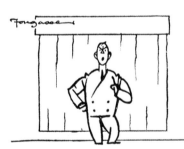

1940. *"When this confounded black-out is ended I'm going to tear down every blind and curtain in the house and make a bonfire in the middle of the road."*

1941. *"When this accursed black-out is over I'm going up on the roof and I'm going to let off all the fireworks and flares and fog-signals that money can buy."*

1942. *"When this filthy black-out finishes I'm going straight round to the Wardens' Post, and I'm going to set fire to it and dance round the flames all night."*

1943. *"When this horrible black-out is lifted I'm going to get up a torch-light procession up and down the High Street, and I'm going to roast a fireguard whole in front of the Town Hall."*

1944. *"When this foul black-out finally goes I'm going to open every window and turn on every light, and I'm going to go round to every house in the Square and ring the bell and shout 'Put that light on!'"*

1945. *"Yes, it's really very nice to see the end of the black-out."*

"Well, perhaps we used to be just a little OVER-ZEALOUS, shall we say, in those early days."

PUNCH

OR

THE LONDON CHARIVARI

Vol. CCVIII   No. 5425

January 10 1945

Charivaria

THERE has been another drop in German morale. They will not be able to dilute it much further.

o   o

There is little improvement in the newsprint situation. Daily papers may not have room till March to print the stories the M.O.I. is keeping back till May or June.

o   o

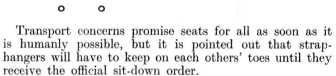

A retired bookmaker is to stand for Parliament. It will be interesting to see if his backers get their place money returned.

o   o

"Paris is full of phoney war correspondents," a press journal asserts. False whiskers, however, cannot hide a really keen fashion expert.

o   o

"What Your Post - War Car Will Be Like," says a heading. A simple way of finding out is to peep under the dust-sheet in the garage.

o   o

Quick Work

"10.57   Carols   [B.B.C. Recording]
10.58   News headlines."—*Radio programme.*

o   o

A radio critic suggests that dance-band leaders should make a New Year resolution not to try to be funny. On the other hand, comedians should continue to persevere.

The Germans have nearly lost their industrial basin. Which means that their big pots are all washed up.

o   o

You 'd-Know-Him-Anywhere Corner

"His forehead was high. On each side of his long nose, whence deep furrows ran to the ends of the mouth, were two black prominent eyes."—*From a novel.*

o   o

Hitler will not return to his mountain retreat. He found even that fastness too slow.

o   o

"It is a thrill for a private soldier to walk out in collar and tie, brown shoes and creased slacks," declares a writer. Particularly if he can collect some salutes from unwary privates with no collar and tie, Army boots and baggy battle-dress trousers.

o   o

Transport concerns promise seats for all as soon as it is humanly possible, but it is pointed out that straphangers will have to keep on each others' toes until they receive the official sit-down order.

o   o

"I should like to buy a jeep from the American Army after the war and tour England in it," says a correspondent. What fun! He could leave the roads to less enterprising motorists and follow the hounds.

"Well, did you have a good time in Rome, Jenkins?"
"Fine, Sir – lovely NAAFI!"

"Keep your eye on that niche up there. The saint in it has got a Tommy-gun"

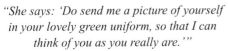

"She says: 'Do send me a picture of yourself in your lovely green uniform, so that I can think of you as you really are.'"

"It appears these were the headquarters of the Hitler Youth."

233

SHUTTING THE DOORS

(By the middle of January, British General Bernard Montgomery and US
General George Patton had stopped the last major German offensives in
Western Europe.)

THE LAST HEIL

Impressions of Parliament

Business Done:

Tuesday, May 8th. — House of Commons: Victory!

Wednesday, May 9th.—House of Commons: The Morrow of Victory.

Thursday, May 10th.—House of Commons: Celebration of Victory.

Tuesday, May 8th.—Members made their way to the Houses of Parliament to-day with the aid of smiling but firm members of the Metropolitan Police. That sentence should not be misunderstood. The only reason for the assistance of the police was the good-humoured crowd of some 30,000 of the citizenry which pressed about the Palace of Westminster, cheering everything and everybody, and generally making a joyful noise.

For this was The Day for which all had toiled, wept, sweated and many had bled, for more than five years. This was Victory in Europe Day— VE Day for short.

For weary weeks, months and years the world had waited for the news that was about to be imparted, and the crowds stood there wedged in front of the home of the Mother of Parliaments, giving three—or more—rousing cheers to each new arrival, and three—or more —not less rousing, when there were no arrivals at all. Flags flew from every window, and a vast Union Jack had been placed at the top of Victoria Tower by Mr. DUNCAN SANDYS, the Minister of Works, whose artistic and enthusiastic eye had seen to the decoration of public buildings.

The Commons assembled to the distant refrain of that Old English ballad: "Roll Out The Barrel!" Members crowded into the Chamber too overjoyed to think of business.

Mr. Speaker arrived, the severity of his uniform relieved by the gold and black robe that appears only on occasions of high State. Sir CHARLES HOWARD, the Serjeant-at-Arms, Mr. ST. GEORGE KINGDOM and Mr. ERIC EDENBOROUGH, his deputies, all wore the lace ruffles and cuffs appropriate to the occasion. Even those austere (if invariably charming and urbane) officers, Mr. "ERIC" METCALFE and Major EDWARD FELLOWES, Clerks of the House, wore their Orders of the Bath about their necks, giving an unwonted splash of splendour to their severely-businesslike Table.

Your scribe has missed no great Parliamentary occasion in the last twenty years, but this was the greatest of them all. The House could not have held another Member. All the gangways were blocked by eager listeners; the benches were packed until they creaked; Ministers, crowded out of their rightful territory on the Front Bench, were glad to creep into the humbler abodes of the back-bencher.

One seat only remained vacant— that right opposite the Dispatch Box on the Government side of the House.

Questions were dutifully ploughed through, with nobody (not even, on this occasion, the questioners) paying any great attention to the answers.

"EVEN THE RANKS OF TUSCANY   "

"For he's a jolly good fellow!"

Over all hung that curious brand of excited jollity found only in the Commons House of Parliament, which takes the form of facetious questions and comments, mostly of such a technical and domestic nature that visitors in the Galleries are left in a state of puzzlement. Now and then, through windows that, a week ago, would have been open for some unrecordable reason, but which can now be "revealed" to have been flung wide to admit the brilliant sunlight, there came the sound of cheering and snatches of song, and more cheering.

Lightheartedness had its decorous fling on the floor of the House, as when Mr. SOMERSET DE CHAIR complained that the war had been over for twelve minutes (he did not make public his method of computation) and some wish of his constituents in Norfolk had not been fulfilled. "Nor," snapped Mr. RUPERT DE LA BERE, from Evesham, "in the Vale of Evesham!"

The rest of the House seemed able to bear these injustices with some calm, and then the bores (and others) had an unexpected and (to them at least) altogether delightful windfall. Questions ended, and it was necessary to keep the business going until that vacant seat by the Table should have its expected occupant.

Even Sir JOHN ANDERSON, the Chancellor of the Exchequer, who jokes "wi' deeficulty," got quite skittish and made several replies that pleased him a good deal and even produced a smile from the easy-to-please House. Lady ASTOR, amid loud cheers, asked a little wistfully that "the barbed wire should be taken down"— but did not say where. Lord WINTERTON wanted the lights turned on on the coast. Mr. "DAVY" KIRKWOOD wanted to know "what we arrrre waitin' on?" That question was the success of the afternoon.

Nobody told him, for in the middle of a pause of complete silence the door opened and the entire House, floor, galleries and all, turned like a Wimbledon Centre Court crowd to look at the man who walked slowly in. The silence, as they say in the Upper House, was "no longer heard." Members rose, jumped on the benches, waved their Order-papers, opened their lungs and just yelled long and loud like schoolboys greeting the hero of the match. For the new ·arrival was the Prime Minister, blushing and grinning like any schoolboy-hero, nodding right and left, shaking hands, fumbling for his notes—and then, quite unaffectedly, taking out a crumpled handkerchief and flicking away a tear that began to trickle down his cheek. Abruptly, as though suddenly remembering its dignity, the House got down from the benches and was silent.

Mr. CHURCHILL went slowly to the Table, announced that it had just been his duty to tell the world of the surrender of Germany and the triumph of Allied arms, and read the text of his broadcast address. All Europe— not least "our dear Channel Islands" —had been freed from the yoke of the tyrant. Unconditional surrender had been received from the German High Command.

Pausing irresolutely, Mr. CHURCHILL turned towards the SPEAKER and uttered the words a world in torment had waited more than 2,000 days to hear: *"The German war, Mr. Speaker, is therefore at an end!"*

"Sorry, but only half-wrapping until we've finished off the Japs."

A roar of cheers that rivalled the efforts of the thirty thousand outside came from the throats of the Great Elected. Raising his voice, Mr. CHURCHILL cried with proud challenge: "Advance, Britannia! Long live the cause of Freedom! God Save The King!"

Startled, the House cheered again, to fall silent as Mr. CHURCHILL paid a husky-voiced tribute to its own steadfastness throughout the war and the manner in which it had preserved the title deeds of Democracy while waging relentlessly the most rigorous war.

Then, regaining some of his old formality, he moved that the House adjourn to the Church of St. Margaret (whose rector, Canon ALAN DON, resplendent in purple and crimson, sat by the door) to give thanks for the deliverance of the world from German domination.

The whole House, Members, officials, Pressmen, Official Reporters, messengers, went through the now silent crowds to Parliament's own church, to take part in as moving a service as even that historic (and sorely bomb-damaged) church has ever witnessed.

The service was part of the Parliamentary proceedings of this memorable day, and duly appeared in Hansard's report. Many an eye was wet in that gathering—wet with tears of pride and joy, at the news, wet with pride and grief as Canon DON read out a startlingly long list of Members of the House who had died on Active Service. The grand words of "The Old Hundredth" rang triumphantly through the church, the service drew to its majestic end, the SPEAKER's procession wound its way through the once more roaring crowd. And (in the words of Hansard's Official Report), "The bells of St. Margaret's Church were rung in celebration of Victory."

Back in the Commons' Chamber Mr. CHURCHILL quietly moved the adjournment. It was the end of a great Day. The longed-for VE Day had passed into Parliamentary history.

Wednesday, May 9th.—Postscript to VE Day: Mr. HERBERT MORRISON, the Home Secretary, announced amid thunderous cheers that Britain is to be liberated—from some scores of the Defence Regulations that have burdened us. It was a characteristic gesture, made with characteristic promptness.

Thursday, May 10th.—Post-postscript to VE Day: The Commons began the Committee stage of the Bill to give Family Allowances to the parents of the children of the nation, the citizens of the future. It seemed the perfect climax to a week of History, an earnest of happier days to come.

o　　o

Useful Hobby

"... took us round this vast preserve containing thousands of casks. They are made

— BY —
THE MARQUIS
OF DONEGALL

of American oak and are sent to Scotland for maturing whisky."—*Sunday Dispatch.*

The Housing Crisis

With 200,000 houses completely destroyed by bombing raids and a further half a million requiring major repairs, alongside the absence of any home construction since 1939, it was clear a major housing crisis would occur at the war's end, especially as the newly demobilised flooded home and family lives were re-established. The Housing (Temporary Accommodation) Act 1944 planned for the building of 300,000 prefabricated houses as a stop-gap solution, though just over half that number were actually built. The notoriously flimsy prefabs were the butt of many *Punch* cartoons.

"Progress or no, somebody'll always crop up with roots in the past..."

"Couldn't we paint some wheels on it or something?"

RED SKY AT MORNING

BREAKERS AHEAD

"For goodness' sake, do try to pull together!"

TROUBLE IN THE QUEUE

"Take your turn, please – there's nothing under the counter for anyone."

THE NEW BOY

Mr R A Butler: *"It may not be very easy at first, but you'll soon settle down."*

FAREWELL

"Since there's no help, come let us kiss and part."

(The war is won, but trouble looms. British industry faces daunting challenges, while the United Nations conference is the scene of territorial disputes. R A Butler's reforming Education Act comes into force, the wartime coalition government is dissolved and and a general election is called.)

THE UNCHANGING FACE OF BRITAIN

"Takes a bit of getting used to, a spot of 'oliday traffic."

"'Ere! 'Oo's supposed to be tellin' their experiences?"

"I thought you'd promised not to try and influence my vote in this election, George."

"Now if my party got in it would mean that a poor little undersized brat like this would have some sort of chance in life."

Demobilisation

Plans for the return of around five million servicemen and women to civilian life were announced in September 1944. Release dates were calculated from age and length of service, though a few with skills essential for reconstruction were given priority, as were married people and those over 50. Departure from the forces began at demobilisation centres, where the new civilians were given a medical examination, a "demob suit", and a railway pass home. For many, however, leaving service life was a drawn out process and there were protests over the slow rate of demobilisation.

"As far as I'm concerned I don't care if I never see another uniform"

"He should get his release in January, unless there's another 'speed-up' – in which case, of course, he will be held back owing to the shortage of men."

"...so I wrote to my MP and finally got back the job I was doing before the war."

"I'm hoping for release under Class B for reconstruction."

Impressions of Parliament

Business Done

Wednesday, August 15th.—House of Lords: His Majesty Opens Parliament.

House of Commons: Thanks are Rendered.

Thursday, August 16th.—House of Commons: The Morning After.

Wednesday, August 15th. — Coincidence, whose long arm has been made to account for such unlikely things, really performed a service to the people of this country to-day, for it decreed that the end of the war (brought about by the surrender of Japan at midnight) and the beginning of the new Parliament should fall on the same day.

This meant that the crowds that milled around the Palace of Westminster had the huge delight of seeing the KING and QUEEN drive to the opening in an open state landau. A ready-made royal pageant "laid on" with astonishing celerity. It was raining heavily, and the crowd cheered extra loudly in appreciation of the pluck of the powder-blue silk-clad QUEEN in refusing to use a closed car, which would have cheated the onlookers of part of their pomp and pageantry.

But, uncomfortable as the journey must have been, their Majesties were unperturbed as they walked slowly into the House of Lords to perform the opening ceremony. Peers, peeresses, newly-elected M.P.s, all crowded in, with two score diplomats sitting in their special "box." This time the ceremony was in its correct setting, the House of Lords' Gilded Chamber, surrendered temporarily—and by no means unconditionally—by the Commons.

The KING put on his gold-braided cap—he was in the uniform of an Admiral of the Fleet—and read the longest Speech from the Throne in recent Parliamentary annals.

It was also the first composed by a Socialist Government with an independent majority. Mr. CLEMENT ATTLEE, the Prime Minister, stood at the Bar with justifiable pride of authorship expressed in his face. Mr. WINSTON CHURCHILL, the Leader of the Opposition, stood by his side, wearing the inscrutable expression proper to a prospective literary critic.

The Speech completed, the KING took the QUEEN's hand, walked slowly out, and was gone—into the cold of the rain and the warmth of the cheers once more.

The moment the KING had gone from the Gilded Chamber, men in shirt-sleeves hurried in and performed a task that would have done no discredit to the expert scene-shifters of Drury Lane. Away went the two golden Thrones and their dais. Away went the diplomats' box, the space where M.P.s had stood. In came long scarlet-covered benches, to form once more the shape of the House of Commons. And—final touch of authenticity—in came the Speaker's Chair, to be hoisted into position—lights, reference books, footstool and all.

All this while Members were getting luncheon.

Then, led by Mr. Speaker in his magnificent black-and-gold robes, and with Mr. ATTLEE and Mr. CHURCHILL following closely, the Commons crossed to St. Margaret's church to render thanks for the coming once more to the stricken world of the blessing of peace.

It was a simple, moving service, conducted by Mr. Speaker's Chaplain, Canon ALAN DON.

NO DIM-OUT
"The lights burn brighter and shine more broadly than ever before."

Then back to the House, through cheering crowds, to hear from Mr. ATTLEE a short speech which was deeply moving and eloquent. He moved an Address of congratulation to the KING on the triumphant ending of the war, and struck just the right note in his references to the part we all—from the Royal Family to the humblest of us—had played in the victory.

Then Mr. CHURCHILL (whom the ranks of Labour Tuscany inexplicably omitted to cheer on this Day of Days) rose and seconded, his voice ringing through the Chamber as he proclaimed the triumph of right over wrong, the victory of the Allied cause. One thing he did not mention was the part he and his Conservative colleagues had played in that event.

Nor, to the general surprise, did anyone else. Unless it was the crowds outside which mobbed Mr. CHURCHILL and Mr. ANTHONY EDEN, and besieged the place with a chant of "We want *Churchill*—we want *Eden!*"

Resolving that the Address be presented to the KING by "the whole House," M.P.s rose and went to join the crowds.

Thursday, August 16th.—It was perhaps inevitable that more than a trace of the morning after the night before (in the nicest possible sense) should have been found in the Commons to-day. Excitement and exaltation on that scale cannot be sustained for long, and it was, in a sense, a relief that we could settle down to what is (perhaps a trifle euphemistically) called "world peace."

But the House was crowded, and those who squeezed in were rewarded by hearing some of the best speeches made in Parliament for years.

Major JOHN FREEMAN, an attractively-spoken bronze-haired newcomer from Watford (an ex-Desert Rat), moved the Loyal Address of thanks for the Speech from the Throne. It was a perfect performance—using the word "perfect" in its strict sense. It made no mistakes, either of etiquette or of matter; it was delivered clearly and brightly—and, above all, it was so patently sincere. It wasn't what he said—but the pleasant way he said it.

Mr. F. T. WILLEY, from Sunderland, seconded in a speech nearly as perfectly delivered, and having the added grace of humour.

Then Mr. CHURCHILL. He was in what is called "crashing form" and showed the House (with its many Members who heard him for the first time) what he could present in the way of oratorical fireworks.

But it was Mr. ATTLEE who (a little unexpectedly) stole the show. He made a speech full of realism, and it was a speech that called for the courage which has always been his outstanding characteristic. It could not have been easy to tell the exultant majority behind him that there would be unemployment under the new Government, that the nationalization of the coal industry would be of great advantage "*in the long run*"—and to put heavy emphasis on those last words.

It was a brave speech, and one that gave the House added confidence in the Prime Minister, even if it did not broaden the smiles of his supporters.

SPOTLIGHT

(Despite Churchill's wartime leadership, voters were suspicious of
Conservative policies. Labour, under Clement Attlee, with its promise of
social reform, wins the election by a landslide.)

"I'm like you – now we 'AVE got peace I can't realise it!"

"I see we're allowed to spread alarm and despondency again."

"I shall celebrate Victory-day by switching over to asparagus."

"Double-breasted blue coat, rolled lapels, grey worsted suit, black shoes, gunner's tie and red carnation."

"It's a new kind of bomb, darling, for the benefit of mankind."

"Quite like peace-time once more, isn't it?"

Hearing it with Fish

NOT long ago in a strange town, happening to fall off my bicycle opposite a fishmonger's, I noticed some fish on the slab and no queue. So I went in. "Is this fish for sale?" I asked.

The fishmonger had the thin look that goes with his trade and the pleasant friendly air habitual with such men. Of all shopkeepers, by and large, you will find fishmongers easily the most courteous and the least disposed to arrogance.

He said yes, it was.

"Can I buy some?" I asked incredulously.

"Certainly," he said. "What would you like?"

"What are these flat things?" I asked him, pointing with my bicycle pump, which I always carry in my hand when cycling, and he explained that they were plaice, adding, quite without prompting, that they were nice and fresh.

"I can see they are," I agreed. "They look most splendid fish. Could I possibly have as many as two, do you think?"

"Why not?" he said; and detecting a note of surprise in his voice I told him that where I came from it was not possible to walk into a shop and buy plaice. Toil and even tears, I explained, and long hours in the broiling sun and the slow shuffle of maimed feet on the merciless pavement went into the business of purchasing plaice in my city, and even then you didn't get plaice, not blooming likely. Plaice, my foot, I said; what you got was barbel or stockfish or a nice bit of bream. You were lucky to get that, I told him, where I came from.

"We've no shortage of fish here," he said. "Shall I fillet them for you?"

I never thought that at my age I should cry openly in a fishmonger's shop, but I confess that when this honest fellow offered to fillet my plaice for me I had to turn my head away for a moment and pretend to be interested in a turbot. I think it was a turbot I was pretending to be interested in, though I am indifferent at the identification of fish. Trim fins, it had, blunt nose, low aspect ratio and the typical white under-surface camouflage of a sea-going fish.

When I turned back again he had filleted one plaice and was getting to work on the second. It is astonishing how quickly a trained fishmonger can fillet. The movements of his knife are almost too swift for the eye to follow, so that the flesh appears to fall away from the bones of its own volition, like butter off a dog's back, as the saying is. He leaves the skeleton so clean and so complete, too, that one feels the fish must have been designed simply to have fillets cut off it.

I said as much to the fishmonger, but he scouted the idea.

"The Lord made 'em to suit 'isself," he said, "not to make life easy for chaps like me. Three and fourpence, that is."

"Why does a fishmonger never overcharge for flat-fish?" I asked, having just thought of a joke.

"Controlled," he said.

"It's a riddle," I explained.

"Riddles!" he said. "I don't go in for riddles much myself. That Hirohito's had it, I see."

"Because it would be more than his plaice was worth."

"Ha," said the fishmonger. "He's a bad hat, if you ask me."

"Who is?"

"That Hirohito. Him and 'is white 'orse. I'd fillet the pair of 'em if I had anything to do with it."

"I'm sure you'd make a good job of it," I said courteously, though to tell the truth I didn't see what Hirohito had to do with my riddle. "Do you think the surrender will come this week?"

"This week!" he said, staring. "Didn't you hear it last night?"

"No," I said. "Hear what?"

"Well, blow me down!" said the fishmonger picking up a halibut (I think) in his amazement and turning it over and over in his hands. "I thought everybody knew by this time. Haven't you heard Mr. Attlee say his piece then?"

"Not a word," I said. "Do you mean to say this is VJ Day?"

"That's right," he said. "It's over." And with a gesture of finality he threw the fish back on the slab.

So, for me, the end of six years of war will always be associated with the soft smack of a halibut on marble. Not an unfitting sound perhaps to symbolize the collapse of the Greater East Asia Co-Prosperity Sphere.

H. F. E.

o   o

One Thing at a Time

"Seaton, against the advice of Supt. C. J. Broughton, refused to ask for time in which to pay the fines and repeatedly asserted that he was not guilty. During the hearing he repeatedly called P.c. Ayres a liar.

On the advice of the clerk, Mr. A. S. Richardson, the Bench decided to leave this question over until cases against other defendants had been heard."—*Local paper.*

o   o

"UNRATIONED Meal, anything eats it, mixed with scraps, dogs, cats, birds. 25s. bag, delivered anywhere."

Advt. in Staffs. paper.

Thanks, no.

THE PRICE OF FLAGS

"Whatever I pay, it will have cost me more than anything I have ever bought before."

DEDICATION
In Memory of the Fallen

PUNCH TIMELINE

1938
Sep 29 Munich Agreement.

1939
Jan National Voluntary Service campaign launched.

Mar 15 Germany occupies Bohemia and Moravia.

Mar 31 Britain and France pledge to support Poland.

Jun 3 Conscription comes into force.

Aug 23 Soviet-German Non-Aggression Pact.

Aug 24 Emergency Powers (Defence) Act (DORA).

Sep 1 Germany invades Poland.

Sep 1 Evacuation of cities begins. First blackout.

Sep 3 Britain declares war on Germany.

Sep 4 British Expeditionary Force (BEF) to France.

Sep 7 National Registration Act introduces identity cards.

Sep 17 Soviets invade Poland.

Oct 6 Polish resistance ends. Phoney War begins.

Nov 3 US Neutrality Act lifts arms embargo.

1940
Jan 8 Food rationing begins.

Apr 11 Germany invades Norway.

Apr 16 British-French Expedition to Norway.

May 10 Winston Churchill becomes Prime Minister. Germany invades Belgium and Netherlands.

May 14 Local Defence Volunteers (LDV) created.

May 17 Germany invades France.

May 28 Evacuation of BEF from Dunkirk begins.

Jun 3 Churchill appeals to US for more arms.

Jun 10 Italy declares war on Britain and France.

Jun 22 French capitulate to the Germans.

Jul 16 Battle of Britain begins.

July 23 LDV renamed the Home Guard.

Sep 7 Blitz begins.

Sep 27 Germany, Italy and Japan sign Three-Power Pact.

Oct 28 Italian invasion of Greece.

1941
Jan 5 Offensive against Italians in Libya begins.

Mar 11 US Lend-Lease Act.

Apr 6 Germany invades Yugoslavia and Greece.

Jun 1 Clothes rationing begins.

Jun 22 Germany invades the Soviet Union.

Aug 14 Atlantic Charter declares Allies' post-war aims.

Sep 16 US Navy patrols protect Allied convoys.

Dec 7 Japan attacks Pearl Harbor.

Dec 8 Japan attacks Hong Kong. US and Britain declare war on Japan.

Dec 11 Germany and Italy declare war on US.

"Now tell us, Frank dear, what are the next moves in the war?"

TIMELINE

Dec 18	All aged 18–60 liable to National Service.	**Dec 2**	Conscription into coal mines announced.	**Mar 27**	Last V-2 attack on London.	
Dec 25	Fall of Hong Kong to Japanese.			**Mar 29**	Last V-1 attack on London.	

Dec 18 All aged 18–60 liable to National Service.

Dec 25 Fall of Hong Kong to Japanese.

1942

Jan 1 United Nations Declaration.

Jan 26 First US troops arrive in Britain.

Feb 15 Fall of Singapore to Japanese.

Jun 21 Fall of Tobruk to Rommel's troops.

Nov 4 British victory at El Alamein.

Nov 8 Allied invasion of North Africa.

Dec 1 Beveridge Report published.

1943

Jan 23 Allied offensive in New Guinea begins.

Jan 31 Germans surrender at Stalingrad.

May 12 Axis Forces in North Africa surrender.

Sep 3 Allied invasion of Italy.

Sep 9 Italy surrenders; German troops fight on.

Dec 2 Conscription into coal mines announced.

1944

Mar 10 R A Butler's Education Act passed.

May 17 Allied Burma offensive begins.

Jun 6 D-Day. Allied landings in Normandy.

Jun 13 First V-1 Flying Bomb (Buzz Bomb) attack.

Jul 21 US landings on Guam.

Aug 4 Allies liberate Paris.

Sep 8 First V-2 Rocket attack on London.

Sep 17 Blackout replaced with "dim-out".

Sep 22 Demobilisation plans announced.

Nov 4 Axis forces in Greece surrender.

Dec 3 Home Guard stood down.

1945

Jan 17 Soviets capture Warsaw.

Feb 7 Yalta Conference.

Mar 27 Last V-2 attack on London.

Mar 29 Last V-1 attack on London.

Apr 1 US invades Okinawa.

Apr 12 Death of President Roosevelt. Truman becomes president.

Apr 23 Soviets enter Berlin.

Apr 25 United Nations Conference begins.

Apr 28 Mussolini captured and executed.

Apr 30 Hitler commits suicide.

May 7 Unconditional German surrender.

May 8 VE (Victory in Europe) Day.

Jun 18 Demobilisation begins.

Jul 5 General election takes place.

Jun 25 United Nations Charter signed.

Jul 26 Labour wins election by a landslide.

Aug 6 Atomic bomb dropped on Hiroshima.

Aug 14 Japanese surrender.

Aug 15 VJ (Victory in Japan) Day. Opening of newly-elected Parliament.

AND YOU MIGHT LIKE TO KNOW...

AFS was the Auxiliary Fire Service (p.17).

Buzz Bombs were V-1 Flying bombs (p.220).

Citizens' Advice Bureaux were founded in 1939 to deal with wartime problems (p.33).

ENSA was the Entertainments National Service Association (founded 1939), providing entertainment to the forces (pp.92, 195)

Lord Haw-Haw was the nickname of an announcer on Nazi English-language propaganda broadcasts (p.58).

NAAFI is the Navy, Army and Air Force Institutes which runs facilities for service personnel (p.232).

National Defence Bonds were part of the War Savings Campaign that sold savings products to the public to raise funds for the war effort (p.60).

Utility products were well-designed consumer goods that used scarce raw materials effectively (p.203).

Woolton Pie was a meatless root vegetable pie named after Food Minister, Lord Woolton (p.126).

Note for purists

We've tried to assemble the very best of *Punch* to tell the story of the Second World War. So where the occasional page of brilliant text had a not-so-brilliant cartoon on it, another has been inserted. The occasional gag cartoon is not in the year it was published, but all political cartoons are, as are the prose pieces (except the one by P G Wodehouse on pp.64–65).

PUNCH
INDEX